THE 7.0%
SOLUTION

*Guaranteed Growth
in a 0.7% World*

DR. WILLIAM A. STACK, RICP, CSA

Published by Best Seller Publishing®, Pasadena, CA
Best Seller Publishing® is a registered trademark
Printed in the United States of America.
ISBN-13: 978-1530317615
ISBN-10: 1530317614

This publication is designed to provide accurate and authoritative information with regard to the subject matter covered. It is sold with the understanding that the publisher is not engaged in rendering legal, accounting, or other professional advice. If legal advice or other expert assistance is required, the services of a competent professional should be sought. The opinions expressed by the authors in this book are not endorsed by Best Seller Publishing® and are the sole responsibility of the author rendering the opinion.

Most Best Seller Publishing® titles are available at special quantity discounts for bulk purchases for sales promotions, premiums, fundraising, and educational use. Special versions or book excerpts can also be created to fit specific needs.

For more information, please contact the author at:
Stack Financial Services LLC
PO Box 503
Salem, MO 65560
or call/text 1(573)247-1116

Alternatively, you may contact the publisher at:
Best Seller Publishing®
1346 Walnut Street, #205
Pasadena, CA 91106
or call 1(626) 765-9750
Toll Free: 1(844) 850-3500

DISCLAIMER

The purpose of this book is to assist consumers in making good *informed* investment choices.

Every investor's situation is unique, and no single product or strategy is fitting for all. The reader is urged to seek personalized advice from his own qualified investment, tax, or legal advisor.

For more information about investing, we recommend www.investopedia.com.

Table of Contents

INTRODUCTION

In the first few weeks of 2016, the stock market had its worst beginning since the Great Depression; over \$6 trillion of value was vaporized from investors' accounts before the end of January. Yet, clients invested in the products and strategies discussed in this book lost nothing. Former Federal Reserve Chairman Ben Bernanke was recently quoted as saying that he did not expect interest rates to normalize back to historical averages in his lifetime, and current Chairwoman Janet Yellen has thus far not contradicted that either in words or actions. The interest rates earned by savers and investors will not normalize back to historical averages unless people learn to save differently than before. This book explains how many people are still earning historically average rates of interest, without risk to their principal, and how you can as well. We will also discuss other pertinent topics, including pending legislation that may affect the way you invest, safe withdrawal rates in retirement, and how alternative assets can help protect you from economic shocks. We believe this information can help change your future quality of life for the better.

CHAPTER 1

INVESTING FOR LIFE

Not very long ago, the worst investment that any American consumer could make was to deposit his money in a savings account at a commercial bank. Almost universally, these accounts paid an interest rate of 5%. There was no minimum deposit amount, and you could withdraw it at any time. Credit unions and savings & loans paid slightly more. Blessed with government insurance, and post-Depression regulations, these investments were absolutely risk-free.

Today, the landscape has changed. Bank deposit rates have declined to near zero, S & Ls have reinvented themselves, and credit unions don't pay much better.

POINT 1: *The reason people invest money is not just to have the money itself, but rather to have a better life.*

Regardless of a person's level of wealth (or lack thereof), financial decisions should be centered on what course of action will make our lives better and not simply on which financial product outperforms the others. The best financial choices can only be made when we consider a person's life situation as opposed to an approach that only considers their financial situation. This approach to financial planning takes a little bit more time in the beginning, but can pay huge dividends in the long run by creating a plan that will not only work today, but also be flexible enough to work tomorrow.

Sometimes, the most appropriate financial advice involves the purchase of non-financial products. Once, when approached by someone "looking for a good place to stow a little money," we advised them not to purchase the highest-paying account, but rather to create a small food stash for themselves, with food costs rising at 24% per year.

This turned out to be excellent advice for them, considering their lack of financial wealth and the small amount of savings they had available to "invest." Incidentally, we also recommend to everyone – even the wealthy among us – to do the same with at least a portion of their savings. Sometimes unforeseen events can happen, either from natural or manmade disasters, which might disrupt the flow of commerce in your region.

In times like these, food and water might be more valuable than cash, gold, or securities, *which you cannot eat.* At the other end of the concern meter, there is a real need and desire to know that your funds are going to last throughout your extended lifetime, which makes successful financial planning and investing a bona fide quality of life consideration. The difference between averaging 4.0% on your money versus 0.40% could become the difference between having a nice restaurant meal 25 times per month versus twice a month. The difference between averaging 4.0% versus losing 40% in a swooning stock market could be even more polarizing. Twenty-five restaurant dinners per month versus a monthly trip to wait in line at the food pantry. Some people can afford to lose 40% without changing their daily lifestyle, because they have enough other resources that they can afford to wait out the economic downturn and will not need to use the funds that have lost ground.

But for many Americans in what we call "Middle America," a 40% loss would soon turn into a 50% loss and more, as they continue to make necessary withdrawals while the market is down. In a short time, they could be in a situation very difficult to recover from that would cause considerable lifestyle changes and a fair amount of angst, affecting many areas of life.

Sometimes, we have clients come in who have stayed with a CD of a certain term, "because that's what we have always done." In one such instance, the income of a retired couple was reduced to $43.75 per month on a principal balance of $159,000. Thankfully for them, alternatives were available that allowed them to increase their income to $346.27 per month without introducing risk to that portion of their portfolio.

So, when thinking about financial decisions and products, what makes these decisions important is not the products or performance themselves, but the ancillary life benefits that such decisions and products make available to us on a daily basis.

POINT 2: *Never base financial decisions or actions solely on what others are doing. Everything is relative.*

There have been times that people would come in and want to invest in something solely because of a report that "Warren Buffett just invested $100 million in this." The problem with this argument is that, while $100 million may sound like a lot of money to many people, for someone like Warren Buffett, it more likely means that he is not overly excited about the investment idea. One hundred million dollars to him would be like $1,000 to many Americans.

When speculating on something because "big-name investors are," just remember that everything is relative.

The same caution is warranted when considering the investment habits of people who may not be as famous or wealthy. Sometimes, the biggest mistakes can be made from trying to follow the advice of friends, neighbors, or relatives who may not be familiar with your situation. At other times, the problem may be that you are not familiar enough with their situation to make an informed decision about whether or not you should be positioning your resources in the same way they are.

Also, the exaggeration syndrome that sometimes plagues fishermen can also plague investors, whereby they talk long and loud about the great return they made on such-and-such investment, but rarely discuss other, similar investments that they lost a significant amount on. Unless someone is an investment or financial planning professional, they are under no obligation to disclose risks or expenses about what they recommend to you, nor are they required to evaluate your situation to determine what may be more appropriate for your goals and circumstances.

POINT 3: *There is no single investment or financial idea that works for everyone all the time. A multi-pronged approach is usually best.*

Every so often, we meet a new client who comes in owning products similar to the ones we offer, but they're not happy about it. Not because the products were bad, but because they were not being used correctly. Sometimes products laden with features such as Income Benefit Riders, or Enhanced Death Benefit Riders are sold to people that don't want or need them, but they pay the fees anyway. Correct implementation of product features is as important as the products themselves. This can only be done when closely considering the personal situation and goals of the investor.

Income Benefit Riders, sometimes called "Lifetime Income Riders" or "Guaranteed Withdrawal Benefit Riders" are features that can be included or added to certain annuity contracts, that guarantee to the owner a level of income they can receive throughout their lifetime. Depending on the company and annuity type, costs can range from 0% to 3.70% to have such a feature. Only those clients who are in need of future income security would find such a feature useful, but many times people who never activate the feature are charged for it anyway. Likewise, Enhanced Death Benefit Riders guarantee to the owner a certain level of death benefit to their heirs, which is higher than the account value itself. This type of feature is only useful to those who have little use for the funds themselves, and who are more concerned for their heirs.

A cookie-cutter plan might be fitting for some, even for most, but that doesn't mean that it's right for you. Any discussion of an investment plan should begin with a basic overview of your life situation and future needs. As such it is rarely, if ever, possible that one financial product can meet all of a client's needs.

Many financial institutions train their sales teamsto "capture all of a client's assets." We have chosen to not take that approach, and instead encourage our clients to place their funds where they will be the most advantageous for *them*. Even if it means they send a portion to the bank down the street. They might have a special need that requires an advisor with special expertise; some specialize in one type of investment product, some another, and we'd be foolish to think we are always the best choice.

Our practice offers products and services in the securities, insurance, precious metals, banking, and tax-planning arenas, but we often encourage our clients to keep some funds in their local bank or credit union; we believe it's the right thing for both us and them to do. Sure, we could always cough up a new product for them to put that money in, but we believe that every investor should set aside a certain amount of funds (and it varies per individual) to be readily available for that occasional emergency. We're good at many things, and your bank is good at others; we don't want to be your ATM. With these types of funds, convenience, not return, is the most important consideration.

For other funds, we believe earning a respectable return is a far more important lifestyle consideration. For example, if a client has funds they are willing to commit for a period of time to earn 0.30%, or 0.70%, or 1.20%, they would be better served for those funds to earn 3.0%, 7.0%, or 12.0%, respectively, in an instrument that protects their principal against losses. The former can be found in any bank lobby. The latter requires the services of a financial consultant, sometimes an independent one.

While there are many financial products and strategies available that claim to average 17% to 20% or more per year, those are not the focus of this book. Rather, we will focus on those solutions that protect principal against losses. In that realm, there are still important choices to be made which can have a large impact upon your current and future lifestyles. Our purpose here is to provide the reader with information about products and services that are available if you or your advisor know where to look. There are reasons, which we will discuss in a later chapter, why they may not offer them to you up front. We will go over that issue in more detail in another chapter, but our hope is that this book will serve as a guide to helping you to earn good returns without unnecessary risk to funds that you cannot afford to lose.

CHAPTER 2

DECIMAL POINT MOVING SERVICES

The numbers you see on your financial statements can make you feel good or bad, depending on where they are in relation to the decimal point. Often new clients come in to see if we can help them change the numbers on their statements. Sometimes we can, other times they are just as happy to keep the same numbers, but move the decimal point over a notch or two.

POINT 1: *Moving Earnings Decimals to the Right Makes People Happy*

We frequently meet retired couples who are accustomed to living on (or supplementing their livelihood with) interest income. The trouble is, over the past several years, their return has plummeted. It could be 0.35% or less, in many cases. By moving the decimal point over one notch, their earnings are increased tenfold to 3.5%, without adding risk to that portion of their portfolio. While 3.5% may not sound like much, when compared to 0.35% on a large amount of money, it makes a significant difference in the lifestyle experienced by the owners of these funds.

POINT 2: *When discussing returns, the most important numbers are to the left of the decimal point.*

Every business uses marketing. In fact, it is considered so important that several undergraduate and graduate business degrees are offered in this subject or as a major sub-component of another business degree.

When you see a large numeral in your return, it can subconsciously improve your opinion of what you have significantly more than it should, based on the position of the numeral relative to the decimal point.

For example, seeing an advertisement for an interest rate of 0.19% makes a much bigger splash than an advertisement for 0.12%, giving the bank or other financial institution a lot of bang for their buck while costing them very little. On a deposit of $10,000 for example, the difference in interest earned over a year's time is only $7. For $7 plus the cost of the marketing, many are persuaded to place funds there instead of down the street for "only" 0.12%. The 9 in 0.19% should not matter much to people, but it often does.

It is far more important to move the decimal point than to change the number. Instead of turning the 0.12% into 0.19% by going down the street, what if you could go up to street and turn the 0.12% into 1.20% by moving the decimal point? Now, instead of a $7 difference, a $101 difference is experienced by the client. When more than $10,000 is involved, that difference is magnified accordingly. The same principle applies to those earning 0.35%. People sometimes spend an hour (or more) of their day to move money from 0.35% at one institution to 0.47% at another institution, for example.

They would be far better off to keep the same numbers but move the decimal point over from 0.35 to 3.50. The amount of time and paperwork involved is very similar to that needed to go to 0.47% but the benefits are nearly 10 times greater. How you can do this is discussed more in Chapter 3, *The 3% Solution*. The same principle can be applied to higher-yielding instruments as well, such as those described in Chapter 4, *The 12% Solution*.

In each case, we often find ourselves helping clients as much or more by moving the decimal point over as by changing the numerals on their statements.

POINT 3: *When discussing expenses, try to move the decimal point to the left.*

So, how can we eliminate risk and help a client achieve an overall average return of about 7% in today's economic environment (Fall 2015)? For one, we seek to lower the expenses (or drag) on a client's investments. Recently, an accountant colleague sent one of his clients to meet with us. This client's previous advisor had placed his money into an investment where the fees consumed ¾ of the earnings each year. Needless to say, this client was not getting ahead. We examined his situation, and found a similar product with much lower expenses. With this change, he quadrupled his take-home earnings without increasing risk. By moving the decimal as far to the left as possible, the impact of expenses can be significant. Sometimes 2.5% expenses can be traded for 0.25% expenses, with the resultant savings showing up as a higher investment return.

One of the benefits of using the financial instruments described in this book is that the expenses associated with them is either zero or nearly so. For those who have been on the rollercoaster mutual find ride, this will be like a breath of fresh air, particularly with regard to expenses. One of the worst things that can happen to an investor is to lose money on the investment *and* pay for the privilege, which could even eat into your principal.

As we saw in the example above, expenses become more impactful as your investment returns get lower. Since this book is about earning conservative returns with guaranteed instruments, it's all the more important to reduce (or even eliminate) the fees. For example, if you own a growth fund that averages 23%, you may not mind paying an annual fee of 1.5%. But if you're earning 5% or less on conservative funds, a 1.5% annual fee becomes unbearable, because it reduces your income by 30% on those funds.

Now, how about a bond fund? Sometimes people own bond funds, while looking for consistent returns with lower volatility than stock funds. A bond fund that earns 3-5% with a 1.5% fee can often be replaced by either a CD or annuity earning similar returns, without the fee, and without the principal fluctuation that comes with bonds. In today's low-interest environment, some analysts believe bonds have a greater-than-normal risk of losing value, which (when combined with high fees) can negate the benefits of monthly interest payments. By lowering the 1.5% fee to 0.15%, or even zero, and removing the chance of losing principal (because it's FDIC-insured), overall returns and peace of mind can be enhanced.

Many of the alternatives out there such as bond funds, variable annuities, conservative stock funds and even some exchange-traded funds (more about these in Chapter 11) can have expense structures that significantly dampen an investor's return in a good year, making their losses much worse in a bad year when their investment has gone down in value *before* the expenses. Often times, simply by changing the financial instrument a person is using, we can help them attain the same return that they would have been happy with otherwise, and eliminate or significantly reduce the expenses.

In this way, we increase the net return on your money. That is, if you invest in a product that advertises a return of (say) 8.2%, you can actually keep that 8.2% payoff (or close to it). When looking at returns, we try to push the decimal point as far as we can to the right.

Who would have thought that something as seemingly insignificant as a decimal point could make such a difference in people's lives? When you look at financial advertisements, or your statements, remember, it's not so much the numerals you are looking at, it the side of the decimal points they appear on, and whether you're looking at an expense or a return. Also, many funds and instruments that openly disclose their expenses may also have behind-the-scenes costs that are *not* disclosed. An example would be the trading costs for some mutual funds; they are not explicit expenses, yet they can decrease your total return by a percent or more per year. If you can get to your desired return with less expense and lower risk and volatility, we believe that may be a better option for some.

I had a retired client, a widow, who brought in a pile of bank and brokerage statements. Her husband had always handled the family finances, and she didn't know what to do. One thing she understood without my help, was that someone (other than herself) appeared to be making money from her accounts. Indeed, she was paying steep monthly fees to the people who managed her money. Which isn't so bad if you're making a decent return, but in her case the expenses exceeded her dividends. Just imagine, paying someone for the privilege of losing your money! In her case, it amounted to a loss of $30,000 to $40,000 per year.

That's a significant expense. Some of it was market-related losses, but a good portion of it was just the cost of owning those investments. By changing the positioning of what she had, we were able to not only ensure that her account would only move up, but we also did away with all of the ongoing expenses. For her, it ended up being a more appropriate strategy that she was much more comfortable with. In fact, she liked it so well that she continued to come and do additional business with us for the next 12 years until she passed away. At that point, her family seemed appreciative that she had plenty of funds for herself, as well as for the family after she was gone. We still work with her children and grandchildren today.

Many fees are disclosed in a prospectus if it's a security; if it's a banking product, they'll have all kinds of fees disclosed when the account is opened; and if it's an insurance product, there will be some disclosures of fees but usually they're in a document that is so long and have so many words in it that few people bother to read the whole thing. They should all be pointed out to the consumer, but sometimes that may not happen.

PROSPECTUS

A prospectus is a legal document, required by the Securities and Exchange Commission, which explains the details (including fees) about an investment offering for sale to the public. Every investor should consult this document, before committing to a particular investment. A prospectus is not required for some MLCDs, annuities, or bank accounts, but other similar disclosures should be consulted for information about them before investing.

Then there are some instruments where there can be undisclosed costs. Besides what a mutual fund prospectus discloses, there could be other trading costs involved with buying and selling stock within the fund, or currency exchange costs in the case of an international fund.

Basically, there may be a lot of places that a client may not realize where fees could be reduced, with net investment performance either being the same or better with less or no expense, and without volatility.

We recommend taking your statements to a financial advisor, or perhaps two or three, and ask them to analyze your accounts. Are your investments in the right places? Are you paying unnecessary fees? For someone who knows where to look and how to find out, it should not take too long. When you find a person who you want to work with, you can then ask them to help make sure you are getting a good value for the expenses you are paying, or if not, perhaps some recommendations about how to decrease expenses and risk, while still earning a good rate.

CHAPTER 3

THE 3% SOLUTION

Earning 3% on excess funds or emergency money used to be so common that it was not necessary to write a chapter in a book discussing how to do it. Today, much of what is available to the average consumer on a traditional time deposit, tying up funds as long as five years and more, pays less than half that rate today. It can be as challenging to safely earn 3% on emergency money as it is to safely earn 12% on longer-term savings resources.

Thankfully, both can be accomplished without introducing stock market risks to your principal. In the next chapter we will discuss how to earn 12%, but in this chapter, we will discuss how to earn 3% on shorter-term funds which is just as important to averaging 7% overall as is earning 12% on your longer-term funds.

POINT 1: *Three percent money is just as important as 12% money.*

Coming up with an average of 7.0% total return on your financial resources is simple math when you know where to place your funds.

There is no single allocation strategy that will work for everyone but as a simple example for illustrative purposes, let's assume that you have half of your funds earning 3% and half of them earning 12%. Your average overall return would be 7.5%. If, however, instead of earning 3%, you earn 0.3% (as many Americans do) on half of your funds, your average overall return would be 18% lower, a significant difference. A more likely scenario is to have approximately 1/4 of your assets averaging 12%, 1/4 averaging 7%, 2/5 averaging 3% and 1/10 averaging less than 3%. In this case, the impact on your overall average return is similar to the previous example, if you exchange 0.3% for 3.0%. Needless to say, earning 3% on a portion of your assets is an important part of *The 7% Solution.*

POINT 2: *"Long-term planning" versus "short-term planning for a long time."*

In order to achieve different results than the average person, we have to think differently about money than the average person does.

While this is certainly true for most of the strategies and results espoused in this book, it is no less true for the concept of averaging 3% on a portion of your assets. The fact that you are reading this book indicates that you are perhaps ready to think differently about your money in order to achieve a different, more beneficial result than the average person. One of the mindsets that we have seen through the years is the tendency of a conservative investor to keep too much money and short-term instruments such as a six-month CD or savings account "just in case we need it" or "in case interest rates rise."

While these may be valid concerns for a short time or with a small amount of money, they become harmful habits when done long term or with too great a portion of assets. We personally own (as do many of our clients) a financial instrument that guarantees to pay a minimum rate of 3% that we can add to at any time and take withdrawals from. After a few years, our withdrawals are unrestricted; that is, we can withdraw any amount we want without paying any fees, while still being able to add funds any time we want, while still earning at least 3% or more on all funds that we place there.

When interest rates rise, the rate on this instrument rises automatically as well. In the 1980s, when prevailing interest rates were much higher, this savings instrument was paying over 12% with no action required by the owner. The rates earned have risen and fallen with prevailing interest rates, but have never been lower than 3%. This continues to be the case today. Even though our withdrawals are limited for a few years, this is a great place to stow some short-term funds for a long time - for as long as we live.

It is comforting to know that no matter what might happen, we will always have a place to stow some funds and earn at least 3% while being liquid enough to withdraw those same funds the next week if necessary. This is in contrast to the thinking of some who are unwilling to commit a portion of their savings to such an instrument because, "Five years is just too long to commit. I want to stay more liquid just in case."

Five years later, often those same people are still sitting with thousands of dollars earning next to nothing on money they have never touched. They will continue to earn next to nothing until they stop thinking short term for a long time and begin planning long term to have a good short-term solution. Even for someone unwilling to commit a significant portion of their savings to a five-year instrument, this strategy can still work in the long run.

For example, let's say you are someone sitting with $50,000 in a savings account earning 0.15% because you are comfortable knowing you can get to your money any time. It would not take a large adjustment to move $5,000 into the five-year instrument paying 3.0% that you can add to at any time and which became liquid at the end of five years. When five years are up, you could at that time add another $40,000 and use that as your primary short-term funding source for as long as you lived, earning a much better rate than before.

Incidentally, the $5,000 earning 3% ($150) will produce more than twice as much interest as the other 45,000 earning 0.15% ($67.50) in a traditional savings vehicle. Please note that even 0.15% is higher than today's average savings account rate of 0.09% (according to bankrate.com), so our illustrations of the advantages of earning 3% are very conservative compared to the current reality.

For the 3% solution, we are talking mainly about funds that you might need to be readily available in an ongoing basis. This requires a two-pronged strategy for maximum effect, using products from the banking industry and the insurance industry.

From the banking industry, you will find there are options available that will pay up to 3 to 4% or even a little more on a fully liquid checking account, with certain restrictions. Those restrictions often include doing a certain number of online or debit card transactions each month, having direct deposit. Or, it might be limited to the first $25,000 or so in that account. This allows you immediate access up to the $25,000 without penalties, while earning 3% or more. Usually, any amount over $25,000 will earn interest at a much lower rate. The other negative aspect of these accounts is that banks can change the rates they are paying on these accounts, knowing that few will move their money to another bank even after they drop the interest rate – so you will want to pay attention to your statements.

For additional funds, you might consider a special type of fixed annuity such as the one I mentioned earlier in this chapter that pays 3% interest and allows you to add money any time, including after the term is up. Many fixed annuities are set up differently, so make sure yours has the necessary features to be a good long-term solution for your short-term funds. One benefit to most fixed annuities is that they boast a minimum guaranteed interest rate, which they cannot go below, unlike the banking industry which can drop rates unexpectedly on demand-type accounts. The drawback to fixed annuities is that during the term, your liquidity is limited to some percentage of the value, say 10% per year for example, without penalty. Thankfully, the annuities we use and recommend for this purpose do not have a prohibitive penalty should an early emergency arise.

In conclusion, I know we have been discussing numbers a lot in this chapter but what we must remember is that numbers and decimal points matter when it comes to the lifestyle we or our families are able to enjoy. No one would want to view their pay stub only to discover that their wages had been reduced by 18%, and yet many Americans with savings are doing just that by allowing their short-term funds to earn considerably less than 3%. In order to safely average 7% overall, a good portion of our short-term funds need to earn 3%.

Thankfully, this is still very possible and is being experienced by those "in the know," which now can also include you!

I met a retired couple who had about $159,000 in savings, and they were accustomed to living on the interest. This was a good plan at the outset, but over time, their return plummeted to about 0.35%. This didn't send them into the poorhouse, but honestly (with such a large principal), they should be able to do much better than $46 a month. We analyzed their situation, and determined that they could benefit from a special type of fixed annuity. With this change, we were able to bump them up to $364 a month in income without adding any risk. For a retired person on a fixed income, $320 extra dollars is pretty big boost.

CHAPTER 4
BANKING BASICS AND FINANCIAL TERMINOLOGY

SAVINGS ACCOUNT. The simplest type of bank instrument is a savings account. Generally, this isn't the place to store the money you need for day-to-day expenses such as groceries and rent. Instead, this is where you accumulate funds for big future needs such as a house, a car, or Junior's college education. Or, perhaps, it can serve as a rainy-day fund for unexpected situations such as major car repairs or medical bills. You deposit the money, and it grows over time. You can make a withdrawal at any time, with no restrictions.

CERTIFICATE OF DEPOSIT. If you're willing to tie up your money for a fixed period of time (at least six months), you can earn a greater return by depositing it in a Certificate of Deposit, or CD. The problem is, these rates have declined precipitously in recent years. People used to be able to walk into a bank, and earn 5% or 6% on a CD. Now, they can only earn 0.3%, 0.4%. Maybe 1.5% if they find a really good one.

But you don't need to settle for a standard CD at the new account's desk in a bank lobby. In the following chapter, we will discuss a different type that offers better returns. These must be obtained from a professionally licensed financial advisor. I'm not talking about fly-by-night outfits or anything. I'm referring to places like ANY MAJOR BANK. We use some of the largest and strongest banks in the country when offering these specialized CDs to our clients, such as Wells Fargo, Goldman Sachs, JP Morgan, BNP Paribas, and Bank of America, among others. Many financial advisors reflexively steer their clients into the stock market. That doesn't work for many, because people can lose half of what they have in a year's time. I don't know if you've ever had anything invested in the stock market, but it goes two ways. It goes up, and it goes down. But if a person could reap a portion of the growth of the market when it is going up, without the losses that happen when the market goes down, that would be the desirable result that these CDs seek to obtain.

GOVERNMENT INSURANCE. During the Great Depression, starting with the stock market crash of 1929, millions of consumers lost their life savings when their banks went broke. But in the years that followed, the federal government enacted a slew of new regulations to stabilize the financial markets. One of these innovations was the establishment of the Federal Deposit Insurance Corporation, or FDIC, which guaranteed the deposits of consumers up to a certain amount (now $250,000). The member banks pay a monthly insurance premium based on the amount of their total deposits, and in return the agency will reimburse any losses suffered by their depositors.

In the 82 years since the formation of the FDIC, hundreds of banks have failed (including 400 following the financial crisis of 2007-2008). But because of the insurance protection they provide, no consumer has lost a penny. You can read more about the FDIC at https://www.fdic.gov/about/history/index.html.

ANNUAL PERCENTAGE YIELD. Let's say that you hold a CD with an interest rate of 5.00%. If your interest is compounded daily (that is, you earn interest on the interest), you might end up with a **yield** of about 5.1267%. Of course, you will earn this yield only if you resist the temptation to withdraw any portion of the deposit.

In order to average 7%, which is the title of the book, we will have some funds earning less than 7%, and will consequently need some funds earning more than 7%, to attain the desired average.

We had a client who hesitated to tie their money up for more than six months or a year at a time. This was a rather extreme case as they had kept their money in a 6-month CD, rolling it over every six months for 20 years. While we always recommend that everyone should have some funds available on a short-term basis or on an immediate basis, such as a savings, or a checking account, or short-term CD. If we have funds that we have not needed to touch for 20 years, that's evidence that perhaps we have too much that's allocated short term. This severely hampered their lifestyle and income over that period of time. As a brief example, using the CD that we referred to just for a 10-year period of time on $100,000 for 6 months, if the 6-month CD average for the last 10 years was 1.3%, gives them an ending value of $113,874.83. Had they chosen to allow that same amount of money to be in an actively managed MLCD, such as the one I'm referring to (that happened to average 21.7%/yr for 10 years), the same $100,000 became $859,012.22. In neither case did they touch their money for 10 years, but what a difference that would make in their lifestyle 10 years later. The principal was protected the same way in both CDs.

We still recommend that clients keep some funds in their local bank, in an account that is readily available to them by check, ATM, or debit card. We also recommend that people have some amount of cash on hand – up to a few thousand, in the event that there is a banking or natural catastrophe, and you need currency for short-term emergency needs.

Principal is considered to be the base amount of money you are putting into an investment. Let us assume that you have $100,000 that you want to invest in something. That is your principal amount. The types of things that we are recommending or informing people of in this book are products that protect their principal. They can't lose what they put in. Unlike the stock market, where you could put in $100,000 today and next week you only have $30,000. If stocks go down, you can lose your principal in addition to earnings. Whereas the products we're talking about are insured or guaranteed, so you can't lose your principal amount. Below is a discussion of options and futures contracts, and ETF's. These are not recommended to be purchased directly, as you might lose value. But we are discussing them here because there are MLCD's available that might use them to produce market-linked interest, while also providing you with FDIC-insured protection.

A STOCK OPTION is a privilege, sold by one party to another, that gives the buyer the right (but not the obligation) to buy ("call") or sell ("put") a stock at an agreed-upon price within a certain period or on a specific date. A stock option might be offered as a reward to an employee who meets certain goals, or attains a certain level of longevity or seniority with a corporate employer.

A COMMODITY FUTURES contract is an agreement to buy or sell a set amount of a commodity (a physical product such as gold, silver, or pork bellies) at a predetermined price and date. Buyers use these to avoid the risks associated with the price fluctuations of the product or raw material, while sellers try to lock in a price for their products. As with all financial markets, others use such contracts to gamble on price movements.

The principle is the same. It's a contract. Let's say I don't want to buy the actual stock, but I want to buy a contract, and the contract allows me to purchase it in the future at a certain price. If I buy the option now and it allows me to buy the stock at $10 in the future and the stock goes up to $20, I can exercise my option and purchase it at $10 and immediately sell it at $20 and make the difference. Or I can purchase a futures contract on the commodities that's based on the price of whatever the commodity is. A commodity is something like grain, it could be corn, it could be pork bellies, it could be oil contracts. I'm buying a futures contract that oil is going to be at a stated price on a fixed date, and I can either lose money or make money with that contract.

ETF is short for *exchange traded fund*. It is a type of investment vehicle that has become a lot more popular in the last five years or so. They're older than that, but they didn't get a lot of traction until recently. What they are is a portfolio of other investment securities that can be traded on the stock exchange, just like a stock can be traded. A mutual fund has a basket of investment securities in it, but you typically can't buy and sell those on the exchange moment by moment. You can put in an order to sell it, but they can't give you the price until the end of the day.

An ETF is also a basket of other securities. For example, you might have an oil ETF and it could have the stocks of Shell, Total (a French company), Phillips 66, or Standard Oil. They could have several of those all in this one ETF, but you can buy and sell that just like you can buy and sell a stock, just at any moment during the trading day. Let's say you want to buy some oil stocks, but you don't know which ones. Yet you feel like oil is a good place to be; the price is going to go up. You can buy an oil ETF and you'll have a portion of several different oil companies.

Let's say it's a utility ETF. In that fund there might be the stocks of a dozen different utility companies, and so you get exposure to the sector without putting all your money in one company. It's a little bit less risky way to invest in an area.

There are ETFs that focus on companies in Norway, or in Europe, or South America, or Asia. If you want exposure to any given market sector, there's probably an ETF out there that will be a diversified way that you can invest in that particular sector.

Again, we do not recommend a novice purchase these products directly, but include this brief discussion as an explanation of the types of securities you might find as the "financial engine" inside of your MLCD or fixed-indexed annuities, which are principal-protected.

CHAPTER 5

THE 12% SOLUTION

Earning 7% overall is generally sufficient for many people to provide necessary income for themselves, while also protecting their financial future from the ravages of inflation, and help accomplish legacy goals of providing for those left behind. This means that both our short-term and long-term savings will have to perform well in order to achieve this.

POINT 1: *We need to earn 12% on some of our money in order to average 7% overall.*

Twelve percent? That seems like an odd number in today's environment when we are talking about principal protected accounts, yet it is not only possible, but essential when considering the overall health of your portfolio. While perusing some business emails this week from some of the vendors we use in our practice, I noticed several offerings from highly-rated banks that offer both high returns and FDIC insurance.

The offering sheet that I was reading lists CDs that use strategies resulting in average returns of 5.5% up to 21.7% APY with terms ranging from 4.75 years to 10 years. Two of these CDs have average returns exceeding the 12% APY that this chapter is about. Just so there's no confusion, the date today as I write this is May 13th, 2015. This may seem unbelievable, but it is absolutely true. I can almost hear you saying what I hear many others say when I tell them things like this: "How is this possible? Why hasn't anyone told me this before?" I will talk about the answer to the first question in this chapter and touch on the second. The second question will be more fully answered in another chapter.

Firstly, how is this possible? A full and complete answer is beyond the scope of this book. The short answer is that powerful financial entities with lots of influence and smart attorneys have received authorization to create "certificates of deposit" that pay rates of interest based on the performance of a market indicator or a combination of market indicators. To be sure, these types of CDs have been around since 1987, have a very consistent and proven track record, and have been used by the wealthy, by municipalities, and by other informed citizens since that time. There are some new developments which we will be discussing later that make some of these CDs even more attractive than they have been in the past.

Sometimes, the performance of these CDs is connected to a basket of common stocks. Sometimes, the interest earned is based on the performance of a basket of commodities contracts. Things such as oil, gold, cocoa, soybeans, et cetera. There are as many varieties of CDs available as there are types of investments available to invest in. Three important distinctions between these CDs versus investing directly in the underlying stocks/indexes/commodities themselves, are liquidity, protection, and return. We will take a look at each of these briefly in turn.

LIQUIDITY. When you purchased a stock, option, futures, or commodities contract directly, you generally can turn around and sell it whenever you want. There is generally not a penalty for selling something five minutes after you purchased it, other than the expenses inherent with selling such investments. Of course, there is no guarantee of the price you will receive when you sell it. You might sell it for either more or less than what you purchased it for to begin with. You generally understand this risk and opportunity when you purchase something like that. If not, you certainly should.

A market-linked CD (MLCD) (also called an equity-linked CD) is connected to the performance of one or more securities or market indexes, such as the S&P 500. While a conventional CD might have a term stated in months, an MLCD carries a term measured in years.

This is also called a type of "structured" investment, which means they are created in order to meet an investor's specific goals. They combine the long-term growth potential of equity or other markets with the security of a traditional CD. The first market-linked CD was offered by Chase Manhattan Bank in 1987, and was used initially by wealthy investors and municipalities. They are available today in smaller denominations, which makes them available to much of the investing public. While some offerings require minimum opening balances of $100,000, as of the time of this writing, many offerings only require $25,000 to get started.

When you purchase an MLCD (market-linked CD), however, your liquidity is more limited. Except in the cases of death or court order, your CD is not guaranteed to return your original amount unless you hold it until maturity. While there are many cases of people cashing in these CDs early without losing any principal, it is not guaranteed. Many MLCDs will pay annual or monthly interest that you are free to spend or save as you will, but the original purchase amount is designed to stay invested until maturity or death, whichever comes first.

Funds that you have a planned need for, say in a six-month timeframe, for example, should not be committed to a high yielding CD that matures in five years. There are times when people keep money rolling over in six-month CDs for 20 years when they would have been far better served to increase their earnings 10-fold or 20-fold simply by lengthening the term and type of CD they were investing in. It is obvious that some did not need access to those funds when they hadn't touched them for 20 years, so this makes it important to have a professional evaluation of your situation before making such an investment.

PROTECTION. Let's talk about the differences in the protection of investing directly versus using an MLCD. When investing directly in investment securities, there are few guarantees other than a reasonable expectation that your order will be executed in a timely manner.

You have no guarantees as to the future value thereof. You might make a little or a lot of money, or you might lose a little or a lot of money. Although, people usually hope to make money investing directly, unfortunately, not everyone does. Sometimes, people lose everything they invest while using these instruments directly. Whereas, when you purchase an MLCD that is FDIC-insured, you take away the opportunity to experience losses as long as you hold it until maturity. If the market or instrument tied to your particular CD crashes, it only means that your earnings, not your principal, are affected.

Many of these types of CDs will often pay a minimum rate of interest comparable to traditional CDs even when the underlying investment itself is negative. For example, one CD might guarantee a return of 0.75% per year as a minimum even if the underlying investment vehicle is down 30%. In a good year, it might pay 6% or 7%, but will always pay at least 0.75%. That compares favorably to a CD that is guaranteed not to be higher than 0.5% or 0.75%, such as is available in every bank lobby across the USA.

RETURN. This is related to the protection issue, but when investing in stocks futures or commodities directly, all of the return minus the expenses necessary to purchase and sell belong to you. All of the losses, unfortunately, also belong only to you. For example, if what you purchased is now down 30% lower than it was when you bought it and you sell it, all you'll have is an amount that's 30% less than what you started with. If it goes down 70%, you've lost 70%. If it goes up 10%, you've made 10%, and it all belongs to you. If, as happens sometimes, you have tripled your money in three weeks, the profit minus what Uncle Sam wants for taxes all belongs to you.

With a market-linked CD, you remove these extremes. You will have none of the losses when held to maturity, no matter what happens in the market. Using a type of CD that we referenced in the previous section that pays a minimum of 0.75% per year, if we assume that the underlying market index for that CD actually went down every year the entire time the CD was in effect, you're still guaranteed to make the 0.75% each and every year. If, on the other hand, there are times when the underlying indexes were up, say 12%, a portion of those earnings – and it varies by

CD, some might have a cap of say 7% – but a significant portion of the earnings belong to you and there is no risk of loss.

POINT 2: *Earning twelve percent consistently is different from earning 12% occasionally.*

What people want is an account that earns 12%, is insured against losses, has no fees, and no time commitment. Of course, this is not possible. There are financial instruments that can accomplish most of these things occasionally, but to earn 12% or more consistently requires a different approach with less liquidity and more time commitment. Sometimes we have to use a little psychology to help clients achieve their goals. This is especially true when dealing with people who have grown accustomed to keeping large sums of money in short-term instruments. One time, a client had kept over $200,000 in six-month CDs, for 10 years, "hoping interest rates would increase". I asked them if they did much traveling, which they did. I asked them if they bought their tickets in advance, or if they mostly bought them at the counter when flying.

They said they save a lot of money by buying their tickets as far in advance as possible, and they rarely, if ever, purchase them at the time of flight. We used their own behavior of committing their funds for a long period of time buying airline tickets to illustrate why they should be more willing to commit more of their short-term funds to a longer-term financial instrument, to vastly increase their overall earnings. Instead of the $26,000 they earned during 10 years (they had averaged 1.3%) in six-month CDs, we showed them other CDs for 5–10 years that would have increased their earnings 8–10-fold over the same time period. This helped convince them to make the changes necessary to sacrifice some liquidity for the sake of earnings.

There are several ways that we can occasionally earn 12% on a principal protected account. We can actually do this with certain types of annuities where your principal is protected and you occasionally earn 12%. We can do this with many types of market-linked CDs where, again, *occasionally* you can earn 12%. But to earn 12% consistently, we have to use a specific type of MLCD.

This is a type of MLCD which is actively managed, whereas many of MLCDs use a fixed basket of securities or commodities to base the performance on. An actively-managed CD sometimes provides the best of all worlds for a certain portion of your assets. Not everyone will be able to commit as much money as they would like to this type of CD for reasons that we will discuss, but first, I want to tell you how a CD can consistently earn 12%.

This is done through a process called "Active Management", and it also uses something new on the investment scene called a "Robo-advisor". This is a concept that's being used by many young people today who don't have a one-on-one financial advisor who they work with, but they may have an app on their smartphone where they invest their money, and it is actively managed. The funds are rebalanced monthly or quarterly, based on their risk tolerance and how aggressive or conservative they want to be with their resources.

With the actively managed MLCD that uses a robo-advisor, phenomenal results have been attained. Unlike those that have a brokerage account with a robo-advisor, these funds are completely insured against principal losses. If, for some reason, the robo-advisor went off the rail and made trades that were all the wrong trades in an FDIC-insured account, the worst that can happen is your return for that month would be less than it would have been otherwise, but your principal is never at risk.

Earlier in the chapter, we mentioned a CD that has averaged over 21% for the last 10 years. I was referring to an actively managed MLCD that uses a robo-advisor to rebalance monthly.

This strategy is used by the largest, strongest, most powerful banking institutions in the country, so it's a proven strategy that wealthy and influential people are using for their own accounts. The same strategies are available to anyone with resources who knows where to look, or who to ask. You will need to use something like this as part of your portfolio. Again, there's no risk of loss to your principal using these instruments, when held to maturity, and they have the best opportunity to provide the growth you need, without risking your principal.

CHAPTER 6
PRODUCTS AND PITFALLS

It would be nearly impossible to construct these portfolios without the help of the securities, banking, and insurance industries. Experience working in each sector has offered us a front-row perspective on the best that each has to offer the American consumer today. Many of the products and strategies espoused by the author can only be achieved by combining the expertise and strengths of each industry, not only within the total portfolio, but sometimes within crucial single products that are offered.

PORTFOLIO: Not too long ago, every investment produced an official document of some kind: a bond, stock certificate, etc. An investor might gather them all into a notebook, or portfolio, for safekeeping. In time, the term *portfolio* came to indicate "the totality of your financial holdings" (which definition fits our purposes pretty well for our discussion in *The 7% Solution*). Today the savvy investor with a home computer can buy and sell a hundred securities in a day, making it pointless to print the certificates. He has no documents in need of storage, yet the designation *portfolio* persists.

The spectrum of products and topics we use in our practice and discuss in this book range from old, proven products and strategies in use since the days of the Roman Empire, to the latest, up-and-coming strategies involving electronic robo-advisors. We believe there is a proper place in every portfolio for products representing each industry, and recommend them all to achieve the desired result of a reasonable return without risking principal, i.e. *The 7% Solution*.

Having said that, the same front-row seat that has helped us spy out the best of the land has also helped us spot other areas in each sector that can cause problems for the average consumer who desires to earn a reasonable return without risking principal. We feel it is appropriate to help shine some light on a few problem areas to help you avoid some heartache and unnecessary losses to you and your family's financial agenda. As we discuss each industry in turn, we will also highlight the particular type of products from that industry that we recommend.

POINT 1: *Choosing the correct product is only half of the battle.*

As we saw in chapter one, there are times when new clients come to us not because they need a different product than what they already have, but because the products they own have not been implemented properly, or have the wrong features activated for their particular needs. This causes them to pay unnecessary fees for services they will never use and frequently did not know they were paying for.

Sometimes this happens because the representative is new and unseasoned. Other times it can happen when the financial company has impressed upon their representatives a motivation or requirement to promote certain products or features, sometimes without regard for the client's needs and circumstances.

In one case, a new client, who happened to be a widow, came in for an evaluation of an account that she had opened recently. She attended a dinner seminar hosted by some attorneys and financial professionals, in which they sold her some trust preparation services and financial products. The products she purchased were very similar to what we would have offered her, except features were added that she did not need. There was no risk of market losses, but there were other problems. She was promised a certain interest rate, but after a couple of years her statements indicated that most of the earnings on her account were being eaten up by fees. Her accountant noticed it while preparing her taxes, and recommended she come talk to us for an evaluation of her current holdings.

We knew as soon as we looked at her statement what had happened. There were special features available on her account that had been turned on from day one that came with specified fees. After a discussion with her about her financial situation and goals, it became obvious that she would never use these features. She also did not remember any discussion of the fees and was concerned further when we told her that similar benefits and features were available on other products that did not charge these fees.

She was sort of trapped at this point. If she stayed in her current account, she would pay fees for something not benefiting her or her family. If she liquidated the account, she would pay fees for getting out. The terms of the account did not allow her to cancel the features and requisite fees that were the problem to begin with. Ultimately, she decided to cut her losses and move to something that was designed to meet her goals without the fees. Sadly, she should have been able to start with that, had someone been listening more closely.

POINT 2: *Every financial product and industry has pitfalls.*

Our experience in the securities, insurance, and banking industries has given us a unique perspective on the strengths and weaknesses of each sector when it comes to products that clients can use. I will try to discuss them all briefly in turn.

SECURITIES: A security is a type of financial instrument (investment) that represents ownership in a company (a stock), a creditor relationship with a corporation or government agency (a bond), or the right to purchase a stock at a future time (an option). Said company or agency is called the issuer.

Again, in every industry there are good and honest people and great products. However, the purpose of this chapter is to identify some of the areas that can cause problems. I'll begin with the securities industry. While many fortunes have been made from investing in securities directly, there are some pitfalls to watch out for. Sometimes I prefer to call this the "insecurities" industry. Sometimes there's corruption that is winked at by regulators at the highest levels, and it seems like legalized theft is par for the course in some sectors. You have a large array of people who are trying to earn money from your money, people who are far removed from the representative or planner who you meet with face to face, or even the robo-planner that you believe is saving you money. It seems that everybody wants a piece of your action.

Of all the financial sectors out there, the securities industry is sometimes the least shy about expecting you to pay for their products and services. They're also not shy about wanting to be paid even when they lose your money. Some good clients we gained (a man and his wife) were from a distinguished investment firm whose representative kept telling them how foolish they were for wanting to get out of the securities they had been in, because they were "making money" (mostly for the firm, the money managers, and the representative).

In this disastrous case, after 16 years of paying fees to the securities industry, the client and his wife were almost back to the amount that they had invested, when they decided to transfer all holdings to our firm. This is one of the worst cases of legal investor abuse I have seen, short of the cases where people lose everything. Sadly, these circumstances are not unique to this case. Even when using no-load funds, there are behind-the-scenes trading costs for each fund that can quickly add up to over 1% a year, not counting the fees that are disclosed.

Another pitfall is what I call "stock market math." What people rarely realize is that when the markets or their financial product goes down 30%, it will have to go back up by 43% just to break even. For example, assume that you have invested $100,000 and the market tanks by 30%, which, by the way, has happened several times in the last couple of decades.

Your holdings are now worth $70,000. If, over the next couple of years, the market or securities product goes up by 30%, your holdings are now worth 70,000 plus 21,000, (which is 30% of 70,000), for a total of $91,000. Just to get back to your original $100,000 requires an increase of 43% on the 70,000. This principle is one of the factors affecting the client who took 16 years to get back almost to where they started. The products we recommend that are associated with the securities industry are MLCDs; in particular, actively-managed MLCDs that invest across several sectors, use a robo-advisor to rebalance monthly, and is FDIC insured. While there are new MLCDs being developed all the time, there are some available currently that have really performed well. Be aware that some results you find will be actual, and some might be "back-tested." Back-tested performance numbers are used when a specific MLCD does not have a long track record (fairly new to the market), but the strategy it uses can be tested hypothetically, to see how it would have done in the past. Be aware that "back-tested" strategies can sometimes be manipulated to do well in the past, but may not necessarily indicate how they will perform in a future, unknown environment. But with FDIC insurance, you cannot lose money when you hold the MLCD to maturity.

In the banking industry, again, there are wonderful people, great products, and solid insurance coverage for people's accounts. However, the banking industry is perhaps the master of hidden fees and what I call the blame game. When you go in to purchase a traditional CD or other banking deposit account, you probably will not pay an explicit fee to buy it or to open the account. Your money will then proceed to earn 3.5 to −4.5 % per year or more. These are the nationwide averages. "What?" you say. You're not earning that much? No, you're probably not.

While your money is earning that much, most of it is harvested for the bank, and you are left with perhaps one tenth of whatever the earnings are. When you complain about only earning 0.3 or 0.4% or less on your deposit product, the explanation you will be given will probably sound something like this: "We're sorry, Mr. or Mrs. Client, but the government is the one that has set the rates so low. As soon as they raise them, we will." While you may not be charged an explicit fee, you're actually losing money every day. Oftentimes the owner of the local bank does not personally purchase most of the products available for sale in their lobby. They purchase products such as what we are telling you about in this book.

The products we recommend most often from the banking industry are: a high-yield checking account with ATM access for operating funds (some of these accounts are available paying 3-4% up to $25,000, with restrictions), and the MLCD. Market-linked CDs are a hybrid product that uses the market services and underlying investments from the securities industry, with the FDIC-insured safety offered by the banking industry. We recommend the specific type mentioned previously in this chapter.

Now we'll move on to the insurance industry. Perhaps no business has provided more financial stability to individuals and the nation through the years than the insurance industry. While few people enjoy paying premiums for any insurance product, millions appreciate the benefits that those premiums provide. Many insurers carried the day during the Great Depression. While many banks were going under, people found that they could keep their money safe by purchasing insurance products of one form or another.

Having said that, there are some things to watch out for and to be aware of. Sometimes insurance companies will design products or add features to products that address concerns people are having. Some concerns are legitimate concerns, which are good problems to solve. Other concerns are somewhat irrational and unlikely to happen but sound scary to the average person. Because of this, sometimes people pay for extra features on their insurance product to put their mind at ease, when in actuality there's very little chance they would activate that feature or benefit from it.

As a case in point, in the last few years, "income benefit riders" have become all the rage. In an era of low interest rates, the income benefit rider is an optional feature to some annuity contracts that guarantees the client a certain level of growth in their future income, say 6 to 8% per year, for a fee ranging from 0.45% to 1.2% per annum.

In other words, let's say a client puts in $100,000 and purchases a 6.5% income benefit rider for a 0.85% fee. This means that when the client decides in the future to begin drawing income from their annuity, they will have the option of turning on the benefits from the income rider. Generally, they will compare their actual contract value at that time to the value of the original $100,000 compounded at 6.5%. Whichever number is higher will be used to calculate their income. If in one year their contract value was $107,000, that value would be used to calculate their income. If, however, in one year their contract value was only $104,000, then $106,500, or the value of the income benefit rider, would be used because it is higher than the $104,000 contract value.

What this means is that the insurance company will then begin paying you an income as if you had $106,500, but you really only have 104,000 in this instance. While they are guaranteeing your income, they may not be guaranteeing you will have any money left in a few years, even though they keep providing the income.

In the meantime, you will still be paying the fees each and every year in some cases. Thankfully, there are products out there that provide income benefit rider features without a fee, which is a great option for people who will probably not use the feature, but it gives them some added assurance they will not run out of income as they get older. Those paying for these features should probably do a little number crunching beforehand to help determine if it is worth the cost to them.

One of the new clients we gained came in with one of these products and was concerned to discover that they were paying 75% of the interest they were earning in fees to pay for the income rider. To add insult to injury, they never actually planned to use this feature. Their main intention was to pass this account on to their children. The fees they were paying ensured that there would be less to give to their beneficiaries. There are many added riders and features available. Some may benefit you more than they would your neighbor, and vice versa. Some, however, seemed to be designed to benefit mostly the insurance company, so be careful to talk to a knowledgeable professional when adding features to your annuity contract.

The types of products we recommend from the insurance industry are: fixed annuities, fixed-indexed annuities, immediate annuities, split annuity strategies, and something called an after-market annuity. An after-market fixed annuity is an annuity that was issued a long time ago, when interest rates were higher. These were often used to secure payouts to someone who won a lawsuit. The company that was sued would sometimes purchase an annuity that would pay out over 10-20 years, with interest rates from 5-8%. Sometimes the person receiving those payments did not want to keep waiting, so they traded their future payments for a lump-sum payment of say, 60-70% of the total value. You may have seen the ads on TV where the guy sticks his head out of the window and shouts, "It's my money and I want it now!" Needless to say, there is a market for these annuities, because they are principal protected, and contractually guaranteed to pay a higher rate than many new annuities.

FRATERNAL INSURANCE COMPANIES. These companies can be a valuable resource for products that can help in your quest to earn 3% (see *The 3% Solution*) on some of your funds. Fraternals are old societal organizations that offered their members insurance and financial products as part of the benefits of membership. Today, many people join fraternals primarily for the insurance and financial products available…

Many fraternal organizations have made their membership and financial products available to any American citizen who desires to join, and many join not for the camaraderie of belonging to a group, but strictly for the financial benefits that come with membership. As not-for-profit organizations, fraternal insurers often support charitable causes with "profits" from the business, but there are no shareholders requiring dividends, and no taxes to pay. This often allows them to pay higher rates to members with funds on deposit. Many of them are as strong as (or even stronger than) their commercial insurance counterparts, and they have a very solid track record of protecting the funds of their members.

Some examples of fraternal organizations include: Foresters, Thrivent Financial, William Penn Association, Modern Woodmen of America, Woodmen of the World, Western Fraternal Life, and many others. Ask them for financial ratings and data to ensure they are strong financially. Many of them are stronger than the average commercial insurer.

As we have seen, there are pluses and minuses to every industry. The main thing to remember is that not every product produced by every industry is necessarily one that you should purchase. As the purpose of this book is to discuss only products that insure your principal, that leaves out many products fromeach industry.

Another thing to consider is the amounts that you are investing. Different industries will insure different amounts, and there are ways to go beyond the maximums in each sector, but all of these things need to be discussed between yourself and the financial professional who you have chosen to work with.

Speaking of that, robo-advisors have their place. We use them, but some of these things will not be available to you from a robo-advisor. You're going to need a knowledgeable person who can help you implement all of these strategies and products, and avoid the pitfalls that exist for the uninformed person who may not be aware of the differences between what will help you attain your goals and what is something that's entirely inappropriate for what you're trying to do.

A no-load fund is a mutual fund that does not impose a sales charge. Many times you can purchase those yourself. If you just call a mutual fund company directly and you want to pick all the funds out, you can do it on your own. Sometimes they're sold by "fee-only planners", who are financial professionals who don't sell products that pay any commissions., but sell you a no-load fund and then add on a fee to manage the account.

No-load funds can be tricky. Even in a fund that does not impose a sales charge of any kind, there are fund administration costs, some that are disclosed and some that are behind the scenes;– not clearly delineated in the prospectus. A no-load fund can still have an annual cost that ranges from 0.1% to over 2%. Then there are behind-the-scenes trading costs. Just the costs of buying and selling the stock that the funds own can quickly add up to over a percent. That's an expense that is also in there, that sometimes people think they're avoiding because they have a no-load fund. But oftentimes there are expenses that they haven't counted on. Sometimes they don't even get the help with the fund or advice to go with it.

CHAPTER 7

WHY DIDN'T THEY TELL ME ABOUT THIS?

This is a big question that has many different aspects to it, but I will try to discuss what I believe are the main reasons in turn. The world operates on money and that is no surprise to anyone who has lived here for more than a few years. In fact, one verse in the Bible says that money answers all things. Some people think that the Bible says money is the root of all evil, but it doesn't really say that. It says that the love of money is the root of all evil.

We can see even from this ancient document that money answers all things or is useful in all things. Yet at the same time, the love of it is the root of all evil. Therein lies the answer to the question posed at the beginning of this chapter. The best financial solutions for clients are not always the best financial solutions for the industries and companies that are providing the financial solutions, strategies, and products available to the investing public. There has to be a certain amount of income derived by the producers of financial products or they will not offer them to the public.

POINT 1: *Sometimes the Back Office Is Steering the Ship*

Occasionally we have someone come in with an account nearly identical to what we could offer them, yet is performing poorly because the representative who sold it to them has activated certain unneeded features of the account, at great expense to the client. Many of these features are designed not so much to benefit the individual client, but to create a consistent revenue stream for the company. In one particular case, a widow was mostly concerned about leaving funds to her children/grandchildren, and had plenty of other income at her disposal – in fact, her checking account grew each month, as she routinely spent less than what came in. Her financial advisor, however, placed her in accounts that were charging her significant fees to promise her a future income stream, while diminishing the amount she could leave to her heirs. But she was not receiving, nor did she want to receive, income from this account. We later discovered that there were many others out there in similar circumstances who had dealings with the same company. This indicates that perhaps their agents are trained to turn on certain features of their accounts as a matter of practice, whether needed or not. The agents did not make more income from these fees, but the company in question certainly did.

There are other cases we have come across where another vendor was duly licensed to offer our clients the same product we did, but was not allowed to, because the company they worked for did not have a corporate agreement with the same companies. The representative was willing to offer it, but was not allowed to.

The issue then becomes, "Where can I find a fair deal, and who will offer it to me?" The question at the beginning of the chapter is, "Why didn't somebody I'm working with tell me?" There are innocent reasons. One reason might be that the representative is fairly new to the industry and may not just be familiar with everything that's available. It's more likely, however, that their hands are somewhat tied, and they may not know not only because they're inexperienced, but because they are restricted by the firm they are working for to only offer certain products or only offer certain types of products.

Another germane reason might be that the person you're working with may not be licensed with a certain industry and can only offer products that are connected to the industry that they are licensed for. The products discussed in this book cover the gamut of the insurance industry, the banking industry, and the securities industry. Without all three, it's difficult to construct a 7% portfolio that is principal protected.

Now, here's an example of the difficulties that we have. I'll use the insurance industry for an example. For many annuities, when interest rates drop, the rates on traditional fixed annuity products are slower to drop than the banking industry. In fact, today, it is still possible to get 3% or 3.5%. Two weeks ago, I met with a client who's still earning a fixed rate of 4% on their insured annuity product. But if you walk into a typical insurance office and asked for a fixed annuity, it's unlikely that you'll earn more than 1% or 2%. It may only be because that person only works for a certain company, or a few companies, and they may not be allowed to sell one that pays a consistent 3% or 3.5%.

I don't mean a gimmick 3%. There are products that might pay you a special rate just for the first year, but then after that, they drop you down to a percent. We don't like to deal with those kinds of products, and don't recommend them in most cases. What I'm referring to are fixed annuities in the insurance industry that are still paying consistently 3%, 3.5%, etc., and are still available for sale.

There are some that have been in business since the 1800s that have never paid less than 3% interest on annuities, such as William Penn, a fraternal insurer, among others. The products that pay like that are still available, but they may not be on your broker's approved product list; and for him, if it's not on the list, it doesn't exist. Perhaps, their company has no corporate agreement with the other company, and so that is one reason why.

Another reason has to do with the income derived from the financial product itself to the people that work in the financial industry. For this example, I will use a financial advisor that might be located in a bank. Now, you could buy the same product from the person who works in the bank or the person down the street at the insurance office, or you could go to an independent financial advisor to buy the same product. They might all be similarly licensed to sell that exact product, but there are reasons why you may not be able to purchase it from anyone except an independent financial advisor. It has to do with the amount of revenue derived from the sale of that product.

Oftentimes, when you are working with an independent financial advisor, there are fewer mouths to feed, so to speak, from the sale of that product. Whereas if you purchased something from an advisor in a banking environment, the fees generated from the sale of that product have to provide an income not only to the representative you're working with, but also to either the insurance industry, or the securities industry, or both, in addition to providing income to the bank itself.

Therefore, sometimes the products that are sold in that environment might have higher costs or higher fees, and even if it's a product which you're not charged a fee explicitly to purchase, the revenue will be subtracted from what the potential earnings are. You could still go to an independent financial advisor and buy a fixed annuity that consistently pays 3.5%. If you walk into the bank or you walk into your brokerage firm, you might only find one that pays you 1% or 2%.

It's not because they're not properly licensed and it's not because they don't know that another annuity exists. It's simply because the place they're working will not allow them to sell it. Because the annuity that pays you 3.5% might pay a low commission, and there's not a lot of money to spread around to so many different parts of the financial industry, so they're not sold. They're not pushed. They're not advertised. Sometimes, you have to find an independent advisor who lives conservatively themselves and is as or more concerned about the success of their clients..

It's the same as it is in many areas of life. When there are more people trying to make a living from the same amount of business, sacrifices are made. In the same way, if you find a good local café that serves good food, many times, you're going to have a better meal at a cheaper price than you might at a chain restaurant where you are providing an income not only to the waitress, and to the cook, and the owner of the restaurant; you're also having to provide income to shareholders of a corporation that is traded on the stock exchange. The more people there are involved with the place where you invest your money, the less likely you are to be told about special deals which make you more likely to make a higher return than the company itself.

We like to work with insurance companies. For example, there is one I have done a lot with that has consistently received awards for customer service and also giving customers a fair shake, paying out as many as $5 of every $6 that they've taken in as revenue. They pay $5 of the $6 they earn into client accounts, which can be a more equitable way than what sometimes happens in the banking industry, where banks take in a revenue on average of 4% to 4.5% on a dollar deposited, but only pay out 4/10 of a percent, and where by and large, most of the return is kept for the bank.

You have to look at where the revenue stream is going and how many people it is trying to support. Sometimes, the reason a financial representative may not tell you about an investment designed to make you more money than the company they work for is that they're not allowed. Sometimes, it's that they may not be properly licensed. But I think one of the main reasons has to do with the amount of fees generated from the products being sold and how many people are involved trying to make a living from the sale of one product.

First of all, you want the people who you're dealing with to earn enough money so they will be there when you need service. Everyone has to make a living, so you're going to pay one way or another. You want the people you're working with to be compensated enough that they're going to be interested in your satisfaction and keeping you as a client, and so that's all a given. Even with that, you want to look at how many people are behind the scenes trying to profit. For example, sometimes firms promote a product that really may not address the needs of a client that well, but it works out really well for the company promoting it.

The representative who is dealing with the public may be completely ignorant of how the product was structured in the back office, and they may not understand the pitfalls, but their hands are tied because their compensation is tied to promoting enough of a certain product. They might get a special bonus or special trip if they sell enough of that particular investment, or CD, or annuity. I know in a local bank, sometimes the people promote a five-year CD that's paying less than 1.5% because they tell the people they can earn a higher interest rate. If the interest rates rise, they're locked in at 1.5%, so that may not be the type of CD you want to lock into.

On the insurance side, it's the same way. Sometimes, a company or a person can make more for themselves by promoting an annuity that guarantees 1% versus one that has a higher guarantee and will pay the client more on average. It is the same way in the securities industry. There are many times when products are promoted by the back office of investment firms, and they might tell the high dividend that might look enticing to a client who is needing income, but what you have to really be careful of in the securities industry is that there may also be risks inherent in that product that haven't been fully grasped by the representative selling it.

They may not even be aware of all of the pitfalls with the product itself. They just promote the dividend, which people are looking for, and then a couple of years later, a person might have received their dividends every month, but the value of their principal might have dropped 30%. The representative might have been paid double to sell that particular product, rather than a comparable product that wasn't quite as volatile. In the meantime, the back office of the securities firm has used that money and made more profit for themselves, and let the losses go to the client.

Unfortunately, that type of behavior happens, and it all goes back to the verses from scripture that we started with. Money is useful in every area of life, but the love of it is the root of all evil. Let the buyer be aware, and know who you're dealing with. You want them to earn a living, but you want them to also place your needs ahead of their own.

Think of the way that extravagant casinos in Las Vegas are built. They're being built because people are generally not making money when they go there. They're losing money. On the local level, sometimes financial institutions will create bigger, and newer, and nicer buildings all the time. Incidentally, in one of the towns that we have an office in, I went to the post office and ran into the owner of one of the banks. They had just built a new banking facility. They had one already, but built a new one.

Just as a matter of conversation, I said, "Hey, your building really looks nice." He laughed and said, "Well, it didn't cost us anything to build that." He said, "We used our customers' money." He laughed and went on in, but there may be some truth to his jesting. The same institution that tells people they cannot give them any higher interest rate somehow can build new buildings. Sometimes, people feel better when depositing their money in a nice building, but they're paying for it whether they know it or not if they're only getting 0.4%. The nicest building may not give you the best return for your money.

Other than that, you can call, check around, and find out what average returns are in an area. If possible, learn something about the people that you're dealing with – outside of the realm that you're dealing with them in. Are they a person who is known in the community? Sometimes, people say, "Well, you should never deal with somebody who earns a commission. You should always deal with somebody who is paid a fee." I'll deal with that in another chapter, but that's not always true.

What you really need is an honest person who's willing to make your success their top priority. They will be paid one way or another, whether it is called a fee, a charge, or a commission. You just want to try to find an honest person who is conscientious with their clients and who has a long-term approach. If they've been in a place for a long time, that's usually a good indicator that they are taking care of people or they wouldn't still be able to be there.

CHAPTER 8

THE FOUR PERCENT RULE

In the last few years, there have been discussions about the appropriate spending rate for retired investors to ensure that an investment portfolio will last throughout their lifetime. The challenges associated with determining an acceptable spending rate have been made more difficult because people are living longer than ever, and their investments are paying near-record low rates. What used to be accepted as universal was a withdrawal rate of 4%, adjusted for inflation from a properly diversified investment portfolio, divided evenly between stocks and bonds. Many analysts have recently called the 4% withdrawal rate into question, explaining that the rate should be lower to compensate for the longer lifespans and low interest rate environment.

The good news is, there are still ways to ensure a safe withdrawal rate of 4% and higher that are guaranteed to provide consistent retirement income throughout your lifetime.

POINT 1: *The experts are right to be concerned.*

As recently as May 2015, there have been articles written in national publications such as the New York Times, US News and World Report, CNBC, and others, calling in to question the veracity of the four percent rule. Some have called for retirees to reduce the portion of their investment portfolio tied to the bond market and fixed income instruments from 50% to 25% of the total to minimize the effects of low interest rates on overall earnings.

This means that the retiree is increasing the equity portion from 50% to 75% of the total to make the average return numbers reach 6 to 7 % per year, from which they can withdraw 4%, according to some. We feel this is a more dangerous approach than is warranted for many investors and fraught with unnecessary and unacceptable levels of risk to attain an income stream throughout retirement. Other financial planners encourage investors simply to reduce the amount of income they take – from 4% down to 2.85%, for example – without modifying the structure of their investment portfolio. While we believe this may help preserve the existence of the portfolio, it also nullifies the reason for having the portfolio by reducing the income stream to the investor.

This is hard to do in the current environment of rising food, energy, and tax-related expenses. Retirees are generally looking for more, not less income. For this reason, we believe a different approach is needed to offer current retirees the ability to withdraw funds at a similar rate to what they're used to, without the levels of volatility and risk presently espoused by some analysts and planners. The original four percent rule was created by Bill Bengan 20 years ago. Bill was a financial planner, now retired, who did some research and calculations to come up with a guideline to determine how much his retired clients could withdraw from their portfolios each year to ensure that their funds would last at least 30 years.

He used a model portfolio evenly divided between stocks and bonds and tested it through every 30-year period from 1926 to 1995. Bill is now following his own advice in retirement by hiring financial planners who still use the four percent rule. He has warned all along, however, that the four percent rule he created is not as certain as the laws of physics and that the way it is implemented may need to be adjusted for extreme conditions. (It is interesting to note, that while Bill is a successfully retired financial planner, he still employs two financial professionals to help him manage his resources to allow him to focus on other aspects of life.) Many believe the conditions of today warrant a change in the implementation of the four percent rule, either by reducing the income from, or increasing the risk to, the original portfolio mix. We believe it is possible to keep the income level the same while reducing risk using the strategies espoused in this book.

POINT 2: *Reduce risk and maintain income in a low interest rate environment.*

How can we reduce risk? One of the premises of this book is that we are using financial instruments that are principal protected. That is, they are protected against losses due to downward market fluctuations. Most people are familiar with a risk associated with the stock market, having seen a portion of their own portfolio drop significantly during times of economic chaos.

S & P 500

The Standard & Poor's company maintains a list of 500 stocks in large companies, which represent the breadth and diversity of the U.S. economy. These companies are chosen by a team of analysts and economists, according to a formula that affords greater weight to corporations with larger market values. The S&P 500 is one of the most widely quoted measures of the health of the American economy. While these stocks are American corporations, a significant portion of their profits comes from overseas sales. So there is also an element of the global economy represented in the health of these American companies.

Since 2000, the stock market (as represented by the S & P 500) has lost about half its value twice, taking double the amount of time to regain the losses as it did to create them. While some financial planners are telling retirees to increase the equity portion of their portfolio to 75%, we believe this exposes the average investor to too much risk. An approximate example would be a $1 million portfolio with $750,000 in the stock market. Losing half of the stock portfolio would bring the portfolio value down from $1 million to $625,000 while still withdrawing $40,000 to $45,000 per year in needed income. Remember, people still need to eat and pay for utilities, taxes, insurance, etc. while the markets are down.

The likelihood of running out of funds early is greatly increased in this scenario, when an investor must continue to withdraw funds in an extended market downturn. By using instruments that do not risk losing principal, the possibility of such catastrophic losses is simply removed from the equation and taken off the table. As we explain more completely in the chapter entitled *The 12% Solution,* there are choices available to today's retiree that enable them to achieve the needed long-term investment returns without the risk of market losses. There is another aspect of risk reduction that we can accomplish by departing from uninsured stock and bond securities.

Besides the normal dangers associated with investing in traditional investment securities, there is an additional hazard that we believe all investors should be concerned about, or at least aware of. It has to do with the lack of experience of the current crop of financial traders and managers on Wall Street. Thirty percent of traders have only been working in the industry for five years or less. Two thirds of the traders currently on Wall Street have never seen a complete fed tightening cycle of interest rates, as it has been nine years since interest rates were raised by the fed in 2006. Many of the senior traders, aged 50 and up, have been replaced either voluntarily or involuntarily for one reason or another.

This situation creates a significant amount of uncertainty concerning how the inexperienced and youthful cadre of securities traders will respond when the ZIRP and NIRP conditions begin to move back towards historical norms. When a few firms have new people on the trading desk, mistakes can be minimized and contained. When an entire industry is being run by newbies, mistakes can quickly become financial catastrophes, affecting clients of every firm. While financial catastrophes could certainly affect the performance of insured financial instruments in the short run, you would have the comfort of knowing that your principal balance was secure and better able to take advantage of improved conditions later with no losses to make up.

As a note, ZIRP, Z-I-R-P is Zero Interest Rate Policy and NIRP, N-I-R-P, is Negative Interest Rate Policy. Those terms describe the interest rate environment we have been in, both recently and for the last several years. These conditions, it is believed, are beginning to change, which can create uncertainty for the traders who have never seen a normal or rising interest rate environment. The second question is: how can we maintain income? There are multiple ways to accomplish this using insured financial instruments available today. One of the simplest ways would be use either a fixed or a fixed-indexed annuity with a lifetime income benefit feature attached.

These are available in a variety of flavors, colors, and fee structures, so be careful to work with a planner who will help you shop for the product or products most suited to your situation. In a nutshell, the income benefit feature ensures that during the accumulation phase, your future income base is growing at a minimum rate (which can be 4% to 8%, depending on the product) while also guaranteeing that your income in retirement will be no less than 4% to 6% of the resulting balance. Again, much depends on the product and the age at which you retire.

Unlike the experience of the original four percent rule retiree, this removes the issue of stock market crashes from the equation as market losses are not possible with these types of financial instruments. The insurance company that issues the policy is contractually obligated to provide a steady stream of income payments not only for 30 years, but for as long as you live. Some payments can be adjusted higher for cost of living or can continue for a spouse. As mentioned before, the benefits and features of each product varies so we recommend working with someone familiar with your situation and current offerings to help ensure you are getting the best fit for you and your family.

Another way to accomplish the same thing is by constructing a retirement portfolio using a combination of fixed annuities, fixed index annuities, and MLCDs, that are FDIC-insured. In this way, you are investing in a variety of instruments that provide similar average return characteristics but without the risks associated with traditional stock and bond investments. By creating an average return of 6 to 7% without losses, you can withdraw a 4% indefinitely without drawing down your funds.

We recommend this approach for larger portfolios and for those who have a goal to leave as much money or more for someone after their death than they are using for themselves and retirement.

For more information on the instruments used to construct a portfolio like this, refer to the chapters entitled *The 3% Solution* and *The 12% Solution*. In the case of the fixed indexed annuity vs. MLCD, both would work for people in every demographic. But for those with higher amounts to insure, we will need to use a combination of products, placed with different companies, to keep all of the funds insured. The annuities are generally more liquid than the MLCDs, and are therefore sometimes more appropriate for someone who can insure all their funds in one account.

This could work for anyone, but with a larger portfolio, they might have more funds than what can be insured by one account. In that case, we would want to split it up and use a variety of different vehicles. For example, if each account was insured to $250,000 and they had a million dollars, we would want to split it up among different instruments to make sure that we're keeping their money safe. We would want to use a variety of different products and companies to make sure that we had the principal protection that we're advertising.

As far as the steady stream of income goes, you could purchase one of the products I refer to in the first section and accomplish it. It's a simple way to do it, but as I mentioned, if someone has a larger account they might have more money than we could insure in just one product.

The zero-interest-rate policies we have experienced lately, leave interest rates at virtually zero or certainly below the rate of inflation. Essentially, people receive no net earnings on their money when they're in traditional deposit products. It also affects the ways that bonds and stocks are traded and how they're affected, because rates are so low and most traders have only seen an environment where rates either were at zero or were decreasing. Two thirds of them have never seen a more normal environment, wherein rates are increased. This is because it's been so long since they increased, a record long time.

Many countries in Europe are actually paying negative rates in some banks, and even in the United States, they're charging people money to deposit their money in their own account. Not only are they not earning very much, they're actually guaranteeing themselves to lose money either on the government bond or in the bank account. This is a crazy environment that's historically not normal, but it's the only environment that many traders on Wall Street have ever experienced. There is talk that there might be increased interest rates at some point.

Some point to the small rate increase of 0.25% we saw in December of 2015, as a hopeful sign of things to come. Personally, I do not think rates can rise much in the near future, but if it does, it will be a new ball game for all of the people who are employed in the financial industry and for many of the traders. If banks suddenly start paying competitive rates on deposits, many investors will perhaps cash out their stocks and bonds.

Traders who are used to seeing the values of securities rise with lowering rates, and who have made certain trades that profit in a no-interest environment, may soon see trading profits vanish or turn negative, as they find it difficult to find buyers for what they need to unload. With everyone running for the exits at the same time, it becomes difficult to estimate what they should be willing to sell for, and how soon valuations might normalize.

CHAPTER 9

FEE-BASED VERSUS FREE-BASED

Currently, there is an agency rule, "The Fiduciary Rule," being considered by the Department of Labor, that seeks to change the way people pay for their investments, and to hold investing professionals to a "fiduciary" standard of placing their clients' needs ahead of their own. While this sounds like a noble goal, the unintended result might be that the public ends up paying fees for what they can currently get for free. In this chapter, we discuss the current models being used by financial professionals, and propose that models that already charge $0 in fees are perhaps a better solution than imposing low fees on everyone.

POINT 1: *All Else Being Equal, Low Cost is Better than High Cost.*

We have gained many clients through the years due to our ability to provide clients with the same or better financial returns, with lower fees. A typical example is when someone brings in statements from elsewhere and says, "It doesn't seem like we are making any money." After reviewing their holdings, we then point out that their accounts are growing, but the growth is being stunted by fees that are either charged up front, or every year, or both. One lady, a widow, was losing 75% of her earnings to various kinds of fees before we showed her how to move her money to a "free-based" account without all the fees, at the same risk level she was in before.

One of the questions that often arises when discussing financial planning and/or financial products has to do with fees and expenses. Not only are the amount of fees brought into question, but also the manner in which they're charged. There are powerful self-interest groups with a lot of marketing and lobbying money to spend on each side of the issue, trying to convince you that their way is best, as well as governmental influences and opinions that seem to change depending on who is in the seats of power and responsibility at any given time. There are two main trains of thought being promoted today which are often in conflict with one another.

There is also another approach, not talked about as much, that we believe offers more value to the average consumer than either of the other two approaches most often seen in the news, which I call "free-based". We will discuss them all in turn.

The old way of doing business, which often gets a bad rap, is the "commission-based model." That is, you discuss your finances with a stockbroker, who then considers your financial situation and recommends some suitable investments with costs involved, wherein he or she is paid a commission in the form of a portion of the costs paid by the client at the point of sale.

This model still exists today. Many investment firms (including one with over 10,000 offices around the country) charge a four- to five-percent upfront sales charge to buy mutual funds, and other fees and commissions for virtually any investment (stock, bond, or CD) that you purchase from one of their brokers. As investments come due, get called (some bonds and CDs are "callable" by the institution that issues them), or it is time to sell a stock that either went up or went down, there will be more commissions and fees paid regardless of whether the client made or lost money on the transactions.

It is because of this possible conflict of interest (where investments might be recommended based on the income to the broker rather than the benefit to the client) that this model has fallen out of favor in many circles. There is currently some momentum at the governmental level to try to change this model or do away with it entirely. Of course there is much resistance to this change, mainly from powerful industry titans that still earn the bulk of their revenues from this method of doing business. To be fair, there are millions of satisfied clients who have been served by this model and who are far better off today from having worked with conscientious financial professionals employed with the sales-charge based fee structure. Many have no desire to learn about the inner workings of financial instruments and are happy to pay a commission or fee to someone else to take care of it.

The other model of compensation most often promoted is "fee based" rather than commission based. As with the commission-based model, there are powerful industry players that are promoting this model as the way of the future to "enhance the client experience," as they say. The proponents of this model say that conflicts of interest are greatly reduced because financial professionals are not compensated based on the number of transactions performed in a client's account, nor by an upfront commission paid when an investment is purchased, but rather by an ongoing fee for helping to manage the money.

A planner using this model might recommend no-load or low-load mutual funds, for example, and then add on a management fee for servicing the account. There are variations to this theme but essentially, you would end up paying a percentage of the account balance every year, payable quarterly or annually. Since there is little financial gain to be made from changing your portfolio to other fee-based investments, the theory goes, you might get advice that is less conflicted than advice you get from someone paid mostly at the time of sale or transaction. While this approach has a high-minded appeal for those not wanting to work with a "salesperson," the end results are not necessarily better (and are sometimes worse) than that of a person served by an honest, commission-based professional.

One thing to remember is that while the purported benefits to the consumer are the most talked about, it is also to the benefit of financial planning firms and non-profit financial education empires that offer credentialing services, to have a steady source of dependable fee income coming in, not subject to the ups and downs of sales. The fees derived from the fee-based model keep coming in year in and year out regardless of whether you are making money or losing money. Whether the planner recommends any changes or not in any given year, the asset-based fees keep on rolling in like clockwork.

If the planner gets lazy, you might not be notified about beneficial changes you should make to your portfolio, since they are being paid whether you make any changes or not. There are also fee-based firms that will charge fees for meeting with you and evaluating your finances each year (or as often as you want to pay for), but will not help implement the recommendations they make. They instead charge by the hour. If you then require the services of another fee-based or commission-based provider to implement the strategies of the hourly-only provider, then there are more fees to be paid each time you go to see them.

Since there are expenses paid directly by the consumer, regardless of whether you call it a commission or a fee, I will refer to them both as fee-based financial services. A hybrid advisor is one that is compensated by both fees and sales charges, paid by the client. The current pending DOL legislation discussed in the introduction to this chapter is being promoted primarily by those who are in the fee-based camp. They would prefer that all financial products be sold in such a way that they can extract ongoing fees from the client, including products that currently do not charge fees. We believe the legislation in its current form will limit the choices and products available to the public unnecessarily, and add costs where there currently are none.

POINT 2: *No-Fee Is Better than Low-Fee*

Recently, we gained a new client who was beginning retirement, because when he called to inquire about the fees involved to speak to us, and the typical costs involved to move his retirement funds to us, I explained that there would be no charge to discuss his finances, and that most likely, there would be no fees he would owe to do business with us. After meeting with us two or three times, he decided to roll over his 401k accounts (scattered among various employers) to us, in part because other people he talked to would have charged him a "low fee", whereas we were charging him "no fee".

Now, I would like to discuss what I call "no-fee" financial planning services. It doesn't get much press (perhaps because not many are aware of it). Just because you are not paying a fee does not make something a good investment. Remember, no one is charging you a fee to purchase a CD at the bank for 0.3%, but you are only receiving 10-15% of the total earnings from your money. The products we recommend in this book are such that the bulk of the revenue earned by your money goes to you. Many of the products currently available that we are discussing in *The 7% Solution* can be purchased without paying sales charges, asset-based fees or hourly fees. To be sure, you can purchase them from many commission-based or fee-based providers and pay an additional fee for using them, or you can contact an independent provider of these products and pay no fees.

We feel that for many people this is an even better model than either of the two that are primarily used by many in the investing public. Chris Anderson wrote a book titled *Free – The Future of a Radical Price* that discusses the many ways that offering a product or service for free is a viable economic model for both businesses and consumers in many fields, including the financial business. While governments and industry lobbyists are currently arguing over the other two models we discussed previously, we believe that the "free" model is perhaps better for the investing public, and fair for the financial professionals working in the industry.

For example, there are many of the fixed annuities or fixed-indexed annuities which the client does not pay a fee to purchase, neither to the insurance company that issues it, nor to the agent who sells it. All of your money goes to work right away on your behalf, without the reduction of sales charges, and also without an annual reduction of fees. The way it works is the insurance company will pay the financial professional for sending them the business, but they will not subtract it from your account. There is often an early withdrawal penalty, but unless you withdraw more than you are entitled to access in any given year, you'll never pay that fee. Careful consideration should be made about how much of your resources you put in these types of accounts, due to the limited liquidity available in them.

In the same way, the CDs that we recommend, specifically the MLCDs, can also be purchased without fees, and without any commission to the independent advisor who recommended them to you. Now, that being said, you can purchase them from a financial services provider who is compensated by one of the other two models we discussed, and pay either a sales charge or asset-based fee to purchase the same thing. We recommend that you seek out an independent financial advisor who is able to offer you these products for greatly reduced costs.

How can they do that? How can an independent advisor offer you the same product for less or no fees? We covered this in Chapter 6, but briefly, an independent advisor may not have extensive overhead, or a large office staff to pay. On the other hand, a stockbroker for a large financial firm might make 30–40% of the income from the fee that's brought in, and then the company takes the other 60–70%. An advisor at a bank might make 25–35% of the revenue, and split the other 65–75% between the bank and investment firm. With an independent advisor, you don't have all those people to take care of. The advisor can still make a good living, and provide you with the same product or service for either less fees, or no fees. You also want to be careful with an insurance-only provider because you will need someone who is also duly appointed and licensed to offer MLCDs to you without charging fees or sales charges. We feel that the only thing better than low fees is no fees.

You should also be aware that you won't find every investment product available at every company. Some specialize in one thing or another, and some may not be familiar with every product, even if their firm offers them. For example, we offer them to people because we are familiar with them, and recommend them where appropriate, depending on each client's situation. Even those working with a different advisor can ask about these products, and sometimes discover that they are available to them. Other times, they may discover that they will need to talk to multiple advisors to use all the products discussed. We generally provide service on all products recommended in this book, and others do as well.

If a CD or bond is "callable," it means that the bank or broker has the option to "call it in" (cancel it) and repay the client. For example, sometimes people buy a 6% 10-year CD that is callable in six months. That means that you are earning 6%, but after six months, the bank can cancel it, and give your money back, forcing the customer to pay another fee to buy a new one. The customer doesn't have that privilege – only the bank that issues it. So when interest rates drop, the bank can get out of their commitment to pay a good rate to the customer, but if interest rates rise, the client is stuck until the 10 years are up. The MLCDs and annuities we recommend are non-callable. That is, the issuing company cannot cancel the features and benefits to the client.

We gained some clients about 12 years ago who were very disillusioned with fees their financial advisor was charging. They were using a hybrid advisor who charged asset-based fees for some accounts, and sales charges for other accounts. Every year they were paying fees, including when they were losing money. After a seesaw experience of making money, losing money, and paying fees without seeing much progress for several years, their accountant suggested they come talk to us. We were able to move them into a "no-fee" strategy using the products we recommend in this book, while also protecting their principal from losses. For the last 12 years, their assets have increased every year (including while in retirement), they have had no losses, and they have paid no fees to us, or to any financial institution we represent. They have continued to recommend our approach, and have sent us more business.

CHAPTER 10

THE WAY FORWARD, AND A WORD ABOUT GOLD

There was a day when the strategies proposed in *The 7 % Solution* were new to the financial world. Between the time they began to be utilized broadly in the marketplace and the time they were initially offered, there were periods of ridicule, opposition, and then full adoption and support. Those who started early have enjoyed the benefits all along. Looking forward, there are some steps that may seem new and untried by most Americans, but what we will discuss in this chapter has a track record which is several thousand years old, and has been employed by people worldwide throughout the centuries.

So far, we have discussed ways that you can bring your investment earnings out of the doldrums without exposing yourself to unwanted market risks. We have discussed ways to earn 3%, ways to earn 12% and higher, and how a blending of these different products and strategies can help you earn an average return of 7% on your money without risking principal in the stock market. This is important as it would enable you to continue to enjoy the 4% rule of withdrawals during retirement, which other investors cannot do without taking on too much risk in their portfolio. We have also discussed ways in which you can minimize expenses, and in some cases, eliminate them, compared to how you might be invested currently. There are some other concerns that I believe we should at least mention as we begin to look not only at what has been working well the last few years, but also at what might become more important in the days and months ahead.

There are some signs on the horizon that indicate new conditions could arise that we may need to prepare for, which go beyond the previously discussed methods of ensuring your financial security.

POINT 1: *The FDIC and the insurance industries can only insure the existence of your money, not the value of your money.*

I was doing some work for some longtime clients recently who had sold some valuable farm land and were looking to preserve not only the cash from the proceeds of the sale, but also the value of what they would ultimately be passing on to their beneficiaries. They had farmed all their lives, but had come to a place in life where taking care of property and livestock was more than they could keep up with and they had nobody living close enough who was interested or able to take on the operations.

They were familiar with the concepts and products we discuss in this book as they had invested money with us in these products 21 years earlier, and had been happy enough with how things turned out that they continued to do additional business with us through the years. While many of their friends had been suffering with ultra-low earnings on their savings (0.3%, etc.), they were happily earning 3–4% minimums on their short-term liquid money all the way through to the present (January 2016) with no principal fluctuations, including through the economic crises of 2001 and 2008, and the steep market corrections this year. They had longer-term funds with us as well that had also performed well for them in the 8–12% range. They are very conservative, and prefer only financial instruments that are insured or guaranteed, either by the FDIC or the insurance industry.

After selling their farming operations, however, we felt it best to discuss something that not only can protect the existence of their money, but also its value. Before, it wasn't so crucial for them as they had plenty of non-financial assets with their farms, livestock, and equipment. After selling out, all they had left were paper assets and cash. While we did purchase more of the same types of accounts and annuities we discuss in this book (which they had owned for a long time and were familiar with), we also purchased some precious metals for them, that is, investment-grade bullion in physical form. Precious metals used to be owned by everyone who had any money at all, since they were part of the makeup of the coins created by our treasury department in common usage. Today the silver has largely been replaced with copper and nickel, and coins that used to be made of nickel or copper have been replaced with cheaper metals such as zinc or steel.

Old nickels from 10 years ago are worth about seven cents if you melt them down for the nickel content, which is 40% higher than the face amount of the coin itself. An old copper penny is worth about twice as much melted down as its face value. The new zinc pennies, not so much. Why is this? Because the government has done a far better job of creating money than they have of protecting its value. Precious metals have done a far better job of preserving value than any paper currency system in the history of mankind.

The FDIC can protect the existence of the dollars you may have in the bank (up to statutory limits of $250,000), but they cannot protect the value of those dollars, that is, what those dollars may buy or be worth in the future. What you were able to buy with $100,000 today, you might be able to buy only half as much of in a few years given the same $100,000. While politicians have changed the definition of inflation (so they can keep saying that it is low), the truth is that common and ordinary expenses paid by average Americans on a daily basis have historically gone up over time. For example, a recent survey showed that the costs for typical breakfast items has risen 24% in the last year, but the official inflation rate is below 2%.

By having an "official inflation rate" that is low, it lowers the COLA adjustments the government pays to government retirees and social security recipients. This tends to harm the finances of individuals but it helps the finances of the government. A simple illustration of the power of precious metals to preserve value over time versus how politicians and people normally try to deal with this issue can be found in the recent national discussion and protests being held about the minimum wage. Many people, politicians, and some municipalities believe that conditions warrant the minimum wage being raised to $15 per hour because a dollar just won't go as far as it used to.

If either the government or the Federal Reserve was effective in their mandate to protect the value of your currency, the "minimum wage" would never have to be raised. The minimum wage has been raised often but it never seems to solve the problem. In 1964, the minimum wage was $1.25 per hour or five silver quarters per hour of work. The melt value of those five quarters is over $20 today. If our currency was still backed by precious metals now as it was then, the minimum wage could still be $1.25 per hour and people could purchase over $20 worth of goods and services for an hour's labor.

As a worker enters the labor market, imagine how pleased he would be to make a minimum wage of $20 an hour without businesses having to raise prices to pay for it. That is what having a stable currency backed by precious metals is like. While we may not be able to convince our governing officials to go back to a gold or silver standard, we can do it ourselves simply by allocating a portion of our resources to investment-grade precious metals. As it is with paper financial instruments, there are some types of precious metals better than others and some strategies and methods of investing in metals that are better than others, so be sure to discuss your situation with an advisor qualified and knowledgeable about working in that sphere. You can always call or respond to the precious metals advertising done on TV, the internet, or radio, but our experience has been that many times people overpay when they don't know what to look for. The types of metals we recommend in our practice are the same types we use ourselves and that our family has been familiar with for the past four generations.

POINT 2: *The world as we know it is changing.*

The world that most of us have known and grown up in is one with the U.S. dollar at the center of most world commerce. This has been slowly changing and is getting closer to a defining moment when as much business will be done without the U.S. dollar as it will with it. This will have an effect on the purchasing power of many Americans who rely only on paper wealth. While there are analysts and commentators on the extreme edges of many issues, often the most reasonable philosophy is somewhere in between the extremes. We believe it is no different when it comes to the future of the U.S. dollar and all paper assets denominated in dollars.

One camp says there is nothing to worry about, the dollar is dominant in world trade and investors should just continue to invest as they always have. This strategy is not working for many, however, with record low interest rates, which is one reason for this book. The camp at the other extreme says that the entire U.S. is about to face a decimating currency collapse from which the U.S. dollar will never recover and that it would behoove people to liquidate all paper investments and purchase precious metals and other tangible assets exclusively.

From our perspective, the most probable outcome and best solution lies somewhere in between these two extreme projections. We believe clients are best served by allocating capital to sectors and instruments that will perform as needed in the short run, while preserving the existence and value of their assets to continue to perform in the long run, no matter what the future may look like. For this reason, we believe precious metals offers an opportunity for those without a lot of tangible assets in their portfolio (farms, rental real estate, businesses, etc.), to protect themselves and their families from what may be a very different world than the one they grew up in.

The right kinds of precious metals can serve as an inexpensive insurance policy against a devalued currency. For example, gold, when I was born (1966), was approximately $35 per ounce. One hundred ounces of gold could be bought for approximately $3,500. If you would have placed $3,500 cash in one box and one hundred ounces of gold in another box and set them aside until today (June 2015), you could view how gold protects the value of your assets better than those entrusted with maintaining the value of our nation's currency. Pulling out those two boxes today, we would find $3,500 currency in one box and the same one hundred ounces of gold in the other, except now the hundred ounces of gold is worth approximately $121,500 as measured in today's currency. How is that for protecting not only the existence but also the value of your resources?

If you deposited the $3,500 cash in a checking account paying zero percent, the FDIC would have protected the existence of the $3,500 currency but not the value of what the $3,500 would buy. Ever since the government decoupled our currency from the backing of precious metals, it has gradually lost purchasing power as this example illustrates. In 1966, $3,500 in currency would purchase one or two nice automobiles. In 2015, $3,500 in currency could purchase an automobile, but $121,500 could purchase several much nicer automobiles. Unlike other financial instruments that offer the potential for price appreciation, such as stocks or mutual funds, gold does not charge fees for sitting in that box for forty years. Zip, nada, none. Capital protection and appreciation without fees, without the risk of losing all the value, in a tax-advantaged status is what gold can do.

Armed with this information, you might be tempted to get rid of all paper investments including the ones recommended in this book and purchase only precious metals. This may not be the best idea however, for a variety of reasons. The title of this book is *The 7% Solution*, and we have laid out for the reader a variety of financial instruments that can protect your principal against losses while delivering a respectable and livable level of earnings. While gold can protect value in the long run, and has throughout every conceivable market condition, it can be volatile in the short run, in either direction. Gold also does not pay interest or dividends, which you may need to supplement your income and which the financial instruments we recommend can readily provide.

As of the writing of this book, gold has averaged a return of approximately 7.31% per year since 1966, or slightly more than 7%. Gold is easy to pass on to your beneficiaries in a tax-advantaged way, is easy to store, has few if any related fees and has a five-thousand-year track record of preserving wealth in all economic conditions. There are short-term anomalies that make gold a good complement to, but not the main component of, an income-based financial plan. The amount and portion of your assets allocated to precious metals is dependent upon individual circumstances, so we recommend speaking with a financial professional who deals with such things. We also believe it is most appropriate when a client's entire financial picture is evaluated and considered in this process.

COLA stands for *cost of living allowance*. People on Social Security are supposed to see an adjustment in their rate of pay each year for inflation, and they call that a COLA adjustment. What happens is the government keeps redefining what the term "inflation" is so they can keep saying it's low and they don't have to give people very much of an increase. In reality, the cost of living goes up a lot more than what they adjust it to for the people. They might say inflation is only 1.2%. When they go to the grocery store, groceries are up twenty percent. Everybody has to eat, so the actual inflation rate experienced by people is usually much higher than what the government says that it is, if that makes any sense.

CHAPTER 11
INSIGHTS AND CONCLUSION

Thus far, we have discussed the challenges that conservative investors and savers have had in the last few years with earning a respectable return without taking unaccustomed risks. We have also discussed some solutions to these challenges that have been available both in the past and in the present. Furthermore, we have addressed how things are changing, what conditions might look like in the not-too-distant future, and what we can do now to prepare for the extended future without jeopardizing our present or near-term future. In this final chapter, we will wrap up by discussing what steps the reader can take to implement some or all of these strategies.

This book was written from the perspective of someone who has worked with the public to develop financial solutions using products and services across a wide spectrum of the financial services industry, as well as wealth management services using tangible assets, for the last twenty-three years. Our perspective is unique, and the performance of the products we have used and recommend has been consistent. As a business owner living in the same area for twenty-four years, we have learned what things are important to our clients. We hope you have found at least one product or strategy that we have discussed enlightening or useful for you or your family.

POINT 1: *The first step might be more accurately described as a series of steps.*

In order to purchase the financial products discussed in *The 7% Solution*, you will want to talk to a financial professional who is properly licensed to offer them, which may involve more than one person. As it turns out, many who are properly licensed are not knowledgeable about these products, nor are they encouraged by their firm to learn about them. Don't be afraid to contact some independent advisors for the purpose of asking questions and gathering information. Take this book along to help you remember what to ask for. To purchase a fixed annuity or fixed-index annuity, you will need to talk to a life insurance agent who is familiar with them. (Not everyone is. Life insurance agents sometimes specialize in one area or another.)

Ask if they are appointed with any "fraternal" life insurance companies. Sometimes a strong fraternal company might offer better terms than a commercial life insurance company, especially in the fixed annuity product line. If they are not appointed to work with fraternals as well as commercials, they may not be considering all the best solutions for you. When it comes to fixed index annuities, your best deals are usually with insurers in the commercial sphere, but features, fees, and performance can vary greatly, so be sure to explain what things are most important to you and ask to see a few different options.

Often an independent agent might have more choices available to choose from than a "captive" agent who can only sell the products of one company. Sometimes a stock broker, bank, investment representative or a fee-based financial planner is also licensed to offer these annuities. Just be careful they do not sell you what is known as a "variable annuity," which does not offer the same protection to your principal (that is, you can lose money if the market goes down). A variable annuity can also have a lot of fees involved that can take away from your investment returns. After-market annuities can be purchased from a duly-appointed insurance agent who knows where to look.

The MLCDs we discussed can also be purchased from either a stock broker, bank investment representative, fee-based financial planner or an insurance agent who is duly appointed as a deposit broker for the banks in question. Be sure to ask about fees to purchase or own these CDs. Sometimes you can purchase the same CD from different channels and one place may charge several hundred dollars to purchase them, whereas another might charge nothing to purchase them. The only thing better than a low fee is no fee, especially when it is to purchase the exact same product, with the same features and issuing institution, etc. Precious metal can be bought from a precious metals dealer or a duly appointed and licensed representative thereof.

Sometimes, as with our firm, you will find this all under the same roof as the other products mentioned, though you may not find that readily. Many financial institutions do not allow their representatives to deal with precious metals because the funds placed there are in direct competition with the other products offered by the institution, which will produce more revenue to the institution. As we discussed somewhat in Chapter 6, there might be various reasons why you might not have heard of some, or all, of these products or strategies before reading this book. It is also possible that even if you have a banker, broker, insurance agent, or fee-based financial advisor that you speak with regularly, some of these products or strategies have never been discussed. If you initiate the discussion, they may either have little knowledge of them or an overly negative opinion.

Recently, there was a stockbroker who responded to one of our informational flyers about MLCDs. He works for the investment advisory division of a large investment bank with a nationwide footprint. Even though the institution he works for offers several MLCDs and makes them available to the public, the broker had little knowledge of the features and benefits, and what type of client might benefit from them or the specifics about how to properly position them in his clients' portfolios. This broker has worked in the financial industry for over ten years in a variety of firms, and in this firm for over three years. Even though they are properly licensed and duly appointed to sell and service such products, by their own admission, they had never done so.

The way that financial institutions make money is either by collecting financial management fees, underwriting securities, or by commissions from the sales of financial products. Even though the financial institution this broker works for offers these products to the public, they do not encourage their sales force (brokers and fee-based advisors) to use them, because the products that are better for the clients do not always pay the most in commissions or residual fee income to the broker or the issuing institution. The broker was encouraged to promote products that were not insured (wherein the client can lose principal) and which produce more revenue for the institution (and the broker). Why would a bank/brokerage firm offer a product they don't want to sell? On the rare occasion someone asks for one, they want to have it on hand. A low-revenue sale and hope for another day is perceived as better than sending the client down the street for good.

You will also find that there are often negative articles in the financial press about some of the most beneficial and useful financial products and strategies available. The reason for this is related to the reasons why many financial intermediaries are unfamiliar with them as well. Financial media, whether in print, television or otherwise, is funded as most other media is funded, that is, by advertising revenue. Large financial institutions are also large sources of advertising revenue. A financial publication or television program prefers to present material that makes their advertisers happy. If they write an article favorable to an FDIC-insured CD that has paid over 10% per year for the last five years, and put it next to an ad for an uninsured mutual fund in which the client can lose 30% in a single year, it might be unhelpful competition.

In like manner, it could be perceived as unhelpful for a publication to do a story on how people are better off earning 3% minimum rates of return on their savings by ditching their savings account, next to an advertisement for a savings account paying a "high yield" of 1.2%. Incidentally, both of these products can be purchased through insurance channels by a duly appointed agent who offers MLCDs and fixed annuities, without paying any fees or going through customary brokerage channels.

POINT 2: *There is a war for your money.*

There's an ongoing rivalry between the securities, banking, and insurance industries, who are all hoping you will place your money with them. What we have attempted to show in *The 7% Solution* is that there is an appropriate place for all of them in your portfolio, but not just any ole products in their lineup. In fact, in order to fulfill the dual mandate of keeping your money safe while earning a respectable return, you will have to request the specific products with certain features as outlined in this book. Don't fall for the fixed annuity that only pays well in the first year and not all years. Don't let the broker sell you a callable CD with fees that you never know how long you will own, or another investment product without FDIC insurance. Don't allow the banker to sell you a regular CD that only pays 0.3% or 1.3%, when you can get one that pays 10% and higher. Now that you know what is available and possible, demand the best. Keep looking until you find someone, or a couple of someones, who can do it for you.

Understand that it may be rare to find one firm or company that is able to offer you all these solutions at one location. Also understand that some advisors would rather sell you something different, something that pays them or their firm more, something that does not insure or guarantee your principal, or something that only protects the existence of your assets but not its value in the future. By using the products and strategies outlined in *The 7% Solution* in an appropriate manner, it is possible to not only have your cake, but to eat it too.

IN CLOSING... with most of 2016 before us, it is natural to begin thinking about what changes may come in the years ahead. The Federal Reserve has recently raised interest rates for the first time in a decade, and many are wondering if they will continue to do so. If so, then what does that do to the information presented in this book? Thus far, the rate increase has done more to help the earnings of financial institutions than the earnings of the investing public. Whether the rates continue to rise or not, it is doubtful that they will rise to levels thought common before the financial crisis of 2008 began. If the recent weakness of the stock market is an indication of what a future of rising interest rates might bring, then using investments that are principal protected (as outlined in *The 7% Solution*) will pay dividends for years to come. Even if conditions are such that an investor cannot quite reach 7% in overall earnings, the fact that you have avoided a 40% loss can be invaluable to your financial future.

It is the author's opinion that with all the geopolitical and economic instability currently in the world, it is likely that further easing of interest rates is more probable than a sustained series of interest rate hikes. Currently, 20-30 countries have negative interest rates, which means when you deposit money at the bank, or buy a government bond, you are guaranteed to receive less than you started with when the investment matures. This is a situation that is unprecedented, and there is not a template in history that world leaders can look to in order to predict how things might turn out.

For these reasons, I would like to reiterate the importance of protecting not only the *existence* of your assets, with insured financial products, but also of protecting the *value* of your assets with precious metals. The Post Office sells what is called a "Forever Stamp" to help mitigate the future devaluation of the American Dollar. It will cost more in the future to purchase a Forever Stamp, but if you still have some you bought at a cheaper price, they will continue to be effectual in getting your letter delivered. We can look at precious metals as "Forever Money" for the same reason. It is interesting to note that the amount of silver needed to purchase a quart of grain in 200 BC is the same amount needed to purchase a quart of grain today, 23 centuries later. Though it requires more American Dollars than it did 50 years ago, it takes the same amount of silver. That is why I call it Forever Money; it has the ability to preserve purchasing power, even from generation to generation. Currency as we know it may change, but the value of precious metals survives through currency changes the world over.

The main purpose of this book is educational, and we hope you have received some ideas to help create a brighter financial future for yourself and your family. In the event that you have more questions, or have been unable to find someone to help you implement the strategies outlined in this book, feel free to contact us directly for further assistance. We have been serving the public in the financial services industry for 24 years, and would be glad to listen to your concerns and offer a few suggestions. You can reach me with a Forever Stamp at P.O. Box 503, Salem, MO 65560, or feel free to reach out on Facebook, Twitter, or email, as you see fit. You can leave a text or voicemail at (573) 247-1116. We will do our best to respond to your inquiries.

ABOUT THE AUTHOR

Bill is a West Point graduate and former Army officer who began a career in financial services in 1992 after completing a tour of duty in the First Persian Gulf War (1990-1991). Since 1992, Bill and his wife Sheri have owned Stack Financial Services, LLC, and offered 360* financial planning services to their clients. Bill has nine years' experience as a Registered Representative in the securities industry, has overseen seven branches in the banking industry as a Senior Financial Consultant, has been a licensed agent in the insurance industry for 22 years, has five years' experience as a Precious Metals Dealer, has trained and worked in the tax-preparation industry since 1994, and is familiar with a wide variety of products and strategies to address specific concerns. Bill has received numerous awards and distinctions, being a top producer (in the top 2%) for various companies, as well as a top producer (in the top 1%) industry-wide, qualifying as a member of the prestigious Million Dollar Round Table organization for many years. Bill has also earned several financial planning-related credentials (RICP(c), CSFP, and CSA), holds multiple licenses in multiple states, and is appointed with multiple carriers. FINRA (Financial Industry Regulatory Authority) recognizes six designations as being "Accredited" in the financial planning industry, and Bill has held "Accredited" and other designations since 2003. He is always learning new strategies, and taking new classes, to better serve clients. Bill has developed a mix of strategies and products that have enabled his clients to earn a respectable return, without losses – including during the last financial crisis, and the long period of low interest rates that has followed.

Bill earned a Bachelor of Science degree in Civil Engineering in 1990, a Master of Theology in 1999, and a Doctor of Practical Ministry degree in 2008. Bill has also completed a variety of courses at The American College of Financial Planning.

Bill's wife, Sheri, earned a B.A. in Accounting, holds the credentials of EA, ATA, and MTA in the field of taxation, is an owner/manager of some H&R Block franchise offices, and has been a Registered Representative in the securities industry for 18 years. She has over 30 years' experience in accounting and taxation. Together, Bill & Sheri work to help minimize the impact of taxes on the financial strategies they employ for their clients. Bill & Sheri both serve on the boards of various community organizations locally and regionally, and assist with fundraising for various charities.

Bill and Sheri have served as Pastors of Salem Full Gospel Church in Salem, Missouri since 2000, and together founded Lifeway Center Inc., the largest food pantry operation in a thirty-county area.